The Logstash Book

James Turnbull

December 22, 2014

Version: v1.4.3 (ad12e18)

Website: The Logstash Book

Contents

List of Figures

Listings

Foreword

Who is this book for?

This book is designed for SysAdmins, operations staff, developers and DevOps who are interested in deploying a log management solution using the open source tool Logstash.

There is an expectation that the reader has basic Unix/Linux skills, and is familiar with the command line, editing files, installing packages, managing services, and basic networking.

NOTE This book focuses on Logstash version 1.2.0 and later. It is not recommended for earlier versions of Logstash.

Credits and Acknowledgments

- Jordan Sissel for writing Logstash and for all his assistance during the writing process.
- Rashid Khan for writing Kibana.
- Dean Wilson for his feedback on the book.
- Aaron Mildenstein for his Apache to JSON logging posts here and here.
- R.I. Pienaar for his excellent documentation on message queuing.
- The fine folks in the Freenode #logstash channel for being so helpful as I peppered them with questions, and
- Ruth Brown for only saying "Another book? WTF?" once, proof reading the book, making the cover page and for being awesome.

Technical Reviewers

Jan-Piet Mens

Jan-Piet Mens is an independent Unix/Linux consultant and sysadmin who's worked with Unix-systems since 1985. JP does odd bits of coding, and has architected infrastructure at major customers throughout Europe. One of his specialities is the Domain Name System and as such, he authored the book *Alternative DNS Servers* as well as a variety of other technical publications.

Paul Stack

Paul Stack is a London based developer. He has a passion for continuous integration and continuous delivery and why they should be part of what developers do on a day to day basis. He believes that reliably delivering software is just as important as its development. He talks at conferences all over the world on this subject. Paul's passion for continuous delivery has led him to start working closer with operations staff and has led him to technologies like Logstash, Puppet and Chef.

Technical Illustrator

Royce Gilbert has over 30 years experience in CAD design, computer support, network technologies, project management, business systems analysis for major Fortune 500 companies such as; Enron, Compaq, Koch Industries and Amoco Corp. He is currently employed as a Systems/Business Analyst at Kansas State University in Manhattan, KS. In his spare time he does Freelance Art and Technical Illustration as sole proprietor of Royce Art. He and his wife of 38 years are living in and restoring a 127 year old stone house nestled in the Flinthills of Kansas.

Author

James is an author and open source geek. James authored the two books about Puppet (Pro Puppet and the earlier book about Puppet). He is also the author of three other books including Pro Linux System Administration, Pro Nagios 2.0, and Hardening Linux.

For a real job, James is VP of Engineering at Kickstarter. He was formerly at Docker as VP of Services and Support, Venmo as VP of Engineering and Puppet Labs as VP of Technical Operations. He likes food, wine, books, photography, and cats. He is not overly keen on long walks on the beach and holding hands.

Conventions in the book

This is an `inline code statement`.

This is a code block:

Listing 1: A sample code block

```
This is a code block
```

Long code strings are broken with ↵.

Code and Examples

You can find all the code and examples from the book on the website or you can check out the Git repo.

Colophon

This book was written in Markdown with a large dollop of LaTeX. It was then converted to PDF and other formats using PanDoc (with some help from scripts written by the excellent folks who wrote Backbone.js on Rails).

Errata

Please email any Errata you find here.

Trademarks

Kibana and Logstash are trademarks of Elasticsearch BV. Elasticsearch is a registered trademark of Elasticsearch BV.

Version

This is version v1.4.3 (ad12e18) of The Logstash Book.

Copyright

© Copyright 2014 - James Turnbull
< james@lovedthanlost.net >

ISBN 978-0-9888202-2-7

9 780988 820227

90000

Version: v1.4.3 (ad12e18)

Chapter 1

Introduction or Why Should I Bother?

Log management is often considered both a painful exercise and a dark art. Indeed, understanding good log management tends to be a slow and evolutionary process. In response to issues and problems, new SysAdmins are told: "Go look at the logs." A combination of `cat`, `tail` and `grep` (and often `sed`, `awk` or `perl` too) become their tools of choice to diagnose and identify problems in log and event data. They quickly become experts at command line and regular expression kung-fu: searching, parsing, stripping, manipulating and extracting data from a humble log event. It's a powerful and practical set of skills that strongly I recommend all SysAdmins learn.

Sadly, this solution does not scale. In most cases you have more than one host and multiple sources of log files. You may have tens, hundreds or even thousands of hosts. You run numerous, inter-connected applications and services across multiple locations and fabrics, both physically, virtually and in the cloud. In this world it quickly becomes apparent that logs from any one application, service or host are not enough to diagnose complex multi-tier issues.

To address this gap your log environment must evolve to become centralized. The tools of choice expand to include configuring applications to centrally log and services like `rsyslog` and `syslog-ng` to centrally deliver Syslog output. Events start flowing in and log servers to hold this data are built, consuming larger and larger amounts of storage.

But we're not done yet. The problem then turns from one of too little information to one of too much information and too little context. You have millions or billions of lines of logs to sift through. Those logs are produced in different time-zones, formats and sometimes even in different languages. It becomes increasingly hard to sort through the growing streams of log data to find the data you need and harder again to correlate that data with other relevant events. Your growing collection of log events then becomes more of a burden than a benefit.

To solve this new issue you have to extend and expand your log management solution to include better parsing of logs, more elegant storage of logs (as flat files just don't cut it) and the addition of searching and indexing technology. What started as a simple `grep` through log files has become a major project in its own right. A project that has seen multiple investment iterations in several solutions (or multiple solutions and their integration) with a commensurate cost in effort and expense.

There is a better way.

Introducing Logstash

Instead of walking this path, with the high cost of investment and the potential of evolutionary dead ends, you can start with Logstash. Logstash provides an integrated framework for log collection, centralization, parsing, storage and search.

Logstash is free and open source (Apache 2.0 licensed) and developed by American developer, Jordan Sissel. It's easy to set up, performant, scalable and easy to extend.

Logstash has a wide variety of input mechanisms: it can take inputs from TCP/UDP, files, Syslog, Microsoft Windows EventLogs, STDIN and a variety of other sources. As a result there's likely very little in your environment that you can't extract logs from and send them to Logstash.

When those logs hit the Logstash server, there is a large collection of filters that allow you to modify, manipulate and transform those events. You can extract the information you need from log events to give them context. Logstash makes it simple to query those events. It makes it easier to draw conclusions and make good decisions using your log data.

Finally, when outputting data, Logstash supports a huge range of destinations, including TCP/UDP, email, files, HTTP, Nagios and a wide variety of network and online services. You can integrate Logstash with metrics engines, alerting tools, graphing suites, storage destinations or easily build your own integration to destinations in your environment.

NOTE We'll look at how to develop practical examples of

each of these input, filter and output plugins in Chapter 8.

Logstash design and architecture

Logstash is written in JRuby and runs in a Java Virtual Machine (JVM). Its architecture is message-based and very simple. Rather than separate agents or servers, Logstash has a single agent that is configured to perform different functions in combination with other open source components.

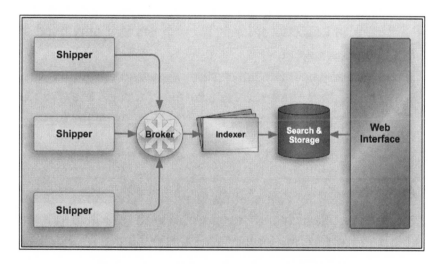

Figure 1.1: The Logstash Architecture

In the Logstash ecosystem there are four components:

- Shipper: Sends events to Logstash. Your remote agents will generally only run this component.
- Broker and Indexer: Receives and indexes the events.

- Search and Storage: Allows you to search and store events.
- Web Interface: A Web-based interface to Logstash called Kibana.

Logstash servers run one or more of these components independently, which allows us to separate components and scale Logstash.

In most cases there will be two broad classes of Logstash host you will probably be running:

- Hosts running the Logstash agent as an event "shipper" that send your application, service and host logs to a central Logstash server. These hosts will only need the Logstash agent.
- Central Logstash hosts running some combination of the Broker, Indexer, Search and Storage and Web Interface which receive, process and store your logs.

NOTE We'll look at scaling Logstash by running the Broker, Indexer, Search and Storage and Web Interface in a scalable architecture in Chapter 7 of this book.

What's in the book?

In this book I will walk you through installing, deploying, managing and extending Logstash. We're going to do that by introducing you to Example.com, where you're going to start a new job as one of its SysAdmins. The first project you'll be in charge of is developing its new log management solution.

We'll teach you how to:

- Install and deploy Logstash.
- Ship events from a Logstash Shipper to a central Logstash server.
- Filter incoming events using a variety of techniques.
- Output those events to a selection of useful destinations.
- Use Logstash's Kibana web interface.
- Scale out your Logstash implementation as your environment grows.
- Quickly and easily extend Logstash to deliver additional functionality you might need.

By the end of the book you should have a functional and effective log management solution that you can deploy into your own environment.

NOTE This book focusses on Logstash v1.2.0 and later. This was a major, somewhat backwards-incompatible release for Logstash. A number of options and schema changes were made between v1.2.0 and earlier versions. If you are running an earlier version of Logstash I strongly recommend you upgrade.

Logstash resources

- The Logstash site (Logstash's home page).
- The Logstash source code on GitHub.
- Logstash's author Jordan Sissel's home page, Twitter and GitHub account.

Getting help with Logstash

Logstash's developer, Jordan Sissel, has a maxim that makes getting help pretty easy: "If a newbie has a bad time, it's a bug in Logstash." So if you're having trouble reach out via the mailing list or IRC and ask for help! You'll find the Logstash community both helpful and friendly!

- The Logstash documentation.
- The Logstash cookbook.
- The Logstash users mailing list.
- The Logstash bug tracker.
- The #logstash IRC channel on Freenode.

A mild warning

Logstash is a young product and under regular development. Features are changed, added, updated and deprecated regularly. I recommend you follow development at the Jira support site, on GitHub and review the change logs for each release to get a good idea of what has changed. Logstash is usually solidly backwards compatible but issues can emerge and being informed can often save you unnecessary troubleshooting effort.

Chapter 2

Getting Started with Logstash

Logstash is easy to set up and deploy. We're going to go through the basic steps of installing and configuring it. Then we'll try it out so we can see it at work. That will provide us with an overview of its basic set up, architecture, and importantly the pluggable model that Logstash uses to input, process and output events.

Installing Java

Logstash's principal prerequisite is Java and Logstash itself runs in a Java Virtual Machine or JVM. So let's start by installing Java. The fastest way to do this is via our distribution's packaging system, for example Yum in the Red Hat family or Debian and Ubuntu's Apt-Get.

TIP I recommend we install OpenJDK Java on your distribution. If you're running OSX the natively installed Java will work fine (on Mountain Lion and later you'll need to install Java from Apple).

On the Red Hat family

We install Java via the yum command:

Listing 2.1: Installing Java on Red Hat

```
$ sudo yum install java-1.7.0-openjdk
```

On Debian & Ubuntu

We install Java via the apt-get command:

Listing 2.2: Installing Java on Debian and Ubuntu

```
$ sudo apt-get -y install openjdk-7-jdk
```

Testing Java is installed

We can then test that Java is installed via the java binary:

Listing 2.3: Testing Java is installed

```
$ java -version
java version "1.7.0_09"
OpenJDK Runtime Environment (IcedTea7 2.3.3)(7u9-↵
  2.3.3-0ubuntu1~12.04.1)
OpenJDK Client VM (build 23.2-b09, mixed mode, ↵
  sharing)
```

Getting Logstash

Once we have Java installed we can grab the Logstash package. Although Logstash is written in JRuby, its developer releases tarball containing all of the required dependencies. This means we don't need to install JRuby or any other packages.

At this stage no distributions ship Logstash packages but you can easily download them from the Elasticsearch site.

TIP If we're distributing a lot of Logstash agents then it's probably a good idea to use Logstash packages.

For our initial getting started we can download and unpack the tarball:

Listing 2.4: Downloading Logstash

```
$ wget https://download.elasticsearch.org/logstash↩
  /logstash/logstash-1.4.2.tar.gz
$ tar zxvf logstash-1.4.2.tar.gz
```

NOTE At the time of writing the latest version of Logstash is 1.4.2.

Starting Logstash

Once we have the tarball unpacked we can change into the resulting directory and launch the logstash binary and a simple, sample configuration file. We're going to do this to demonstrate Logstash working interactively and do a little bit of testing to see how Logstash works at its most basic.

Our sample configuration file

Firstly, let's create our sample configuration file. We're going to call ours sample.conf and you can see it here:

Listing 2.5: Sample Logstash configuration

```
input {
  stdin { }
}

output {
  stdout {
    codec => rubydebug
  }
}
```

Our `sample.conf` file contains two configuration blocks: one called `input` and one called `output`. These are two of three types of plugin components in Logstash that we can configure. The last type is `filter` that we're going to see in later chapters. Each type configures a different portion of the Logstash agent:

- inputs - How events get into Logstash.
- filters - How you can manipulate events in Logstash.
- outputs - How you can output events from Logstash.

In the Logstash world events enter via inputs, they are manipulated, mutated or changed in filters and then exit Logstash via outputs.

Inside each component's block you can specify and configure plugins. For example, in the `input` block above we've defined the `stdin` plugin which controls event input from STDIN. In the `output` block we've configured its opposite: the stdout plugin, which outputs events to STDOUT. For this plugin we've added a configuration option: codec with a value of rubydebug. This outputs each event as a JSON hash.

NOTE STDIN and STDOUT are the standard streams of I/O in most applications and importantly in this case in your terminal.

Running the Logstash agent

Now we've got a configuration file let's run Logstash for ourselves:

Listing 2.6: Running the Logstash agent

```
$ cd logstash-1.4.2
$ bin/logstash agent --verbose -f sample.conf
```

NOTE Every time you change your Logstash configuration you will need to restart Logstash so it can pick up the new configuration.

We've used the logstash binary from our download directory. We've specified three command line flags: agent which tell Logstash to run as the basic agent, --verbose which turns on verbose logging and -f which specifies the configuration file Logstash should start with.

TIP You can also specify a directory of configuration files using the -f flag, for example -f /etc/logstash will load all the files in the /etc/logstash directory.

Logstash should now start to generate some startup messages telling you it is enabling the plugins we've specified and finally emit:

Listing 2.7: Logstash startup message

```
Pipeline started {:level=>:info}
```

This indicates Logstash is ready to start processing logs!

TIP You can see a full list of the other command line flags Logstash accepts at http://logstash.net/docs/latest/flags.

Testing the Logstash agent

Now Logstash is running, remember that we enabled the stdin plugin? Logstash is now waiting for us to input something on STDIN. So I am going to type "testing" and hit Enter to see what happens.

Listing 2.8: Running Logstash interactively

```
$ bin/logstash agent --verbose -f sample.conf
output received {:event=>#<LogStash::Event:0↩
  x3ca2a090 @cancelled=false, @data={"message"=>"↩
  testing", "@timestamp"=>"2013-08-25T17:27:50.027↩
  Z", "@version"=>"1", "host"=>"maurice.example.↩
  com"}>, :level=>:info}
{
    "message" => "testing",
    "@timestamp" => "2013-08-25T17:27:50.027Z",
    "@version" => "1",
    "host" => "maurice.example.com"
}
```

You can see that our input has resulted in some output: a info level log message from Logstash itself and an event in JSON format (remember we specified the debug option for the stdout plugin). Let's examine the event in more detail.

Listing 2.9: A Logstash JSON event

```
{
    "message" => "testing",
    "@timestamp" => "2013-08-25T17:27:50.027Z",
    "@version" => "1",
    "host" => "maurice.example.com"
}
```

We can see our event is made up of a timestamp, the host that generated the event maurice.example.com and the message, in our case `testing`. You might notice that all these components are also contained in the log output in the `@data` hash.

We can see our event has been printed as a hash. Indeed it's represented internally in Logstash as a JSON hash.

If we'd had omitted the `debug` option from the `stdout` plugin we'd have gotten a plain event like so:

Listing 2.10: A Logstash plain event

```
2013-08-25T17:27:50.027Z maurice.example.com ↵
  testing
```

Logstash calls these formats `codecs`. There are a variety of codecs that Logstash supports. We're going to mostly see the `plain` and `json` codecs in the book.

- plain - Events are recorded as plain text and any parsing is done using `filter` plugins.
- json - Events are assumed to be JSON and Logstash tries to parse the event's contents into fields itself with that assumption.

We're going to focus on the `json` format in the book as it's the easiest way to work with Logstash events and show how they can be used. The format is made up of a number of elements. A basic event has only the following elements:

- @timestamp: An ISO8601 timestamp.
- message: The event's message. Here `testing` as that's what we put into STDIN.

- @version: The version of the event format. This current version is 1.

Additionally many of the plugins we'll use add additional fields, for example the stdin plugin we've just used adds a field called host which specifies the host which generated the event. Other plugins, for example the file input plugin which collects events from files, add fields like path↵ which reports the path of the file being collected from. In the next chapters we'll also see some other elements like custom fields, tags and other context that we can add to events.

TIP Running interactively we can stop Logstash using the Ctrl-C key combination.

Summary

That concludes our simple introduction to Logstash. In the next chapter we're going to introduce you to your new role at Example.com and see how you can use Logstash to make your log management project a success.

Chapter 3

Shipping Events

It's your first day at Example.com and your new boss swings by your desk to tell you about the first project you're going to tackle: log management. Your job is to consolidate log output to a central location from a variety of sources. You've got a wide variety of log sources you need to consolidate but you've been asked to start with consolidating and managing some Syslog events.

Later in the project we'll look at other log sources and by the end of the project all required events should be consolidated to a central server, indexed, stored, and then be searchable. In some cases you'll also need to configure some events to be sent on to new destinations, for example to alerting and metrics systems.

To do the required work you've made the wise choice to select Logstash as your log management tool and you've built a basic plan to deploy it:

- Build a single central Logstash server (we'll cover scaling in Chapter 7).

- Configure your central server to receive events, index them and make them available to search.
- Install Logstash on a remote agent.
- Configure Logstash to send some selected log events from our remote agent to our central server.
- Install Logstash Kibana to act as a web console and front end for our logging infrastructure.

We'll take you through each of these steps in this chapter and then in later chapters we'll expand on this implementation to add new capabilities and scale the solution.

Our Event Lifecycle

For our initial Logstash build we're going to have the following lifecycle:

- The Logstash agent on our remote agents collects and sends a log event to our central server.
- A Redis instance receives the log event on the central server and acts as a buffer.
- The Logstash agent draws the log event from our Redis instance and indexes it.
- The Logstash agent sends the indexed event to Elasticsearch.
- Elasticsearch stores and renders the event searchable.
- The Logstash web interface queries the event from Elasticsearch.

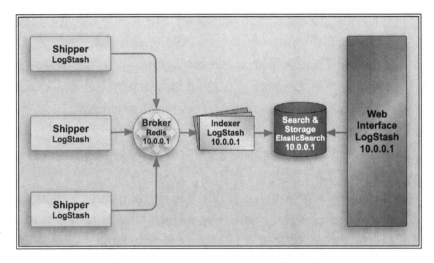

Figure 3.1: Our Event Lifecycle

Now let's set up Logstash to implement this lifecycle.

Installing Logstash on our central server

First we're going to install Logstash on our central server. We're going to build an Ubuntu box called smoker.example↩ .com with an IP address of 10.0.0.1 as our central server.

Central server

- Hostname: smoker.example.com
- IP Address: 10.0.0.1

As this is our production infrastructure we're going to be a bit more systematic about setting up Logstash than we were in Chapter 1. To do this we're going to use the available Logstash packages.

TIP There are other, more elegant, ways to install Logstash using tools like Puppet or Chef. Setting up either is beyond the scope of this book but there are several Puppet modules for Logstash on the Puppet Forge and a Chef cookbook. I strongly recommend you use this chapter as exposition and introduction on how Logstash is deployed and use some kind of configuration management to deploy in production.

Install Logstash

First let's install Logstash. To do so we need to add the Logstash APT repository to our host. Let's start by adding the appropriate GPG key for validating the packages.

Listing 3.1: Adding the Elasticsearch GPG key

```
$ wget -O - https://packages.elasticsearch.org/GPG↵
  -KEY-elasticsearch | sudo apt-key add -
```

Now let's add the APT repository configuration.

Listing 3.2: Adding the Logstash APT repository

```
$ sudo sh -c "echo 'deb https://packages.↩
  elasticsearch.org/logstash/1.4/debian stable ↩
  main' > /etc/apt/sources.list.d/logstash.list"
```

TIP If we were running on a Red Hat or a derivative we would install the appropriate Yum repository. See the agent install later in this chapter for Red Hat installation steps.

We then run an `apt-get` `update` to refresh our package list.

Listing 3.3: Updating the package list

```
$ sudo apt-get update
```

And finally we can install Logstash itself.

Listing 3.4: Installing Logstash via apt-get

```
$ sudo apt-get install logstash
```

Now let's install some of the other required components for our new deployment and then come back to configuring Logstash.

Installing the contributed plugins

In addition to the Logstash package there are also a number of plugins contributed from the community available. We can install them using the `plugin` command.

Listing 3.5: Installing the contributed plugins

```
$ cd /opt/logstash/bin
$ sudo bin/plugin install contrib
```

This will install the community contributed plugins into the same location as the core plugins. You can find a full list of the available contributed plugins on GitHub at https://github.com/elasticsearch/logstash-contrib.

Installing a broker

As this is our central server we're going to install a broker for Logstash. The broker receives events from our shippers and holds them briefly prior to Logstash indexing them. It essentially acts as a "buffer" between your Logstash agents and your central server. It is useful for two reasons:

- It is a way to enhance the performance of your Logstash environment by providing a caching buffer for log events.
- It provides some resiliency in our Logstash environment. If our Logstash indexing fails then our events will be queued in Redis rather than potentially lost.

We are going to use Redis as our broker. We could choose a variety of possible brokers, indeed other options include AMQP and 0MQ, but we're going with Redis because:

- It's very simple and very fast to set up.
- It's performant.
- It's well tested and widely used in the Logstash community.

Redis is a neat open source, key-value store. Importantly for us the keys can contain strings, hashes, lists, sets and sorted sets making it a powerful store for a variety of data structures.

Installing Redis

We can either install Redis via our packager manager or from source. I recommend installing it from a package as it's easier to manage and you'll get everything you need to manage it. However, you will need Redis version 2.0 or later. On our Debian and Ubuntu hosts we'd install it like so:

Listing 3.6: Installing Redis on Debian

```
$ sudo apt-get install redis-server
```

On Red Hat-based platforms you will need to install the EPEL package repositories to get a recent version of Redis. For example on CentOS and RHEL 6 to install EPEL:

Listing 3.7: Installing EPEL on CentOS and RHEL

```
$ sudo rpm -Uvh http://download.fedoraproject.org/↩
  pub/epel/6/i386/epel-release-6-8.noarch.rpm
```

And now we can install Redis.

Listing 3.8: Installing Redis on Red Hat

```
$ sudo yum install redis
```

NOTE If you want the source or the bleeding edge edition you can download Redis directly from its site, configure and install it.

Changing the Redis interface

Once Redis is installed we need to update its configuration so it listens on all interfaces. By default, Redis only listens on the 127.0.0.1 loopback interface. We need it to listen on an external interface so that it can receive events from our remote agents.

To do this we need to edit the /etc/redis/redis.conf (it's /etc/redis.conf on Red Hat-based platforms) configuration file and comment out this line:

Listing 3.9: Changing the Redis interface

```
bind 127.0.0.1
```

So it becomes:

Listing 3.10: Commented out interface

```
#bind 127.0.0.1
```

We could also just bind it to a single interface, for example our host's external IP address 10.0.0.1 like so:

Listing 3.11: Binding Redis to a single interface

```
bind 10.0.0.1
```

Now it's configured, we can start the Redis server:

Listing 3.12: Starting the Redis server

```
$ sudo /etc/init.d/redis-server start
```

Test Redis is running

We can test if the Redis server is running by using the redis↩ -cli command.

Listing 3.13: Testing Redis is running

```
$ redis-cli -h 10.0.0.1
redis 10.0.0.1:6379> PING
PONG
```

When the `redis` prompt appears, then type `PING` and if the server is running then it should return a `PONG`.

You should also be able to see the Redis server listening on port 6379. You will need to ensure any firewalls on the host or between the host and any agents allows traffic on port 6379. To test this is working you can telnet to that port and issue the same `PING` command.

Listing 3.14: Telneting to the Redis server

```
$ telnet 10.0.0.1 6379
Trying 10.0.0.1...
Connected to smoker.
Escape character is '^]'.
PING
+PONG
```

Elasticsearch for search

Next we're going to install Elasticsearch to provide our search capabilities. Elasticsearch is a powerful indexing and search tool. As the Elasticsearch team puts it: "Elasticsearch is a response to the claim: 'Search is hard.'". Elasticsearch is easy to set up, has search and index data available RESTfully as JSON over HTTP and is easy to scale and extend. It's released under the Apache 2.0 license and is built on top of Apache's Lucene project.

When installing the Elasticsearch server you need to ensure you install a suitable version. The Elasticsearch server version needs to match the version of the Elasticsearch client that is bundled with Logstash. If the client version is 1.1.1 you should install version 1.1.1 of the Elasticsearch server. The current documentation will indicate which version of Elasticsearch to install to match the client.

TIP Logstash also has a bundled Elasticsearch server inside it that we could use. To enable it see the embedded option of the elasticsearch plugin. For most purposes though I consider it more flexible and scalable to use an external Elasticsearch server.

Installing Elasticsearch

Elasticsearch's only prerequisite is Java. As we installed a JDK earlier in this chapter we don't need to install anything additional for it. Unfortunately Elasticsearch is currently not well packaged in distributions but it is easy to download packages. The Elasticsearch team provides tar balls, RPMs and DEB packages. You can find the Elasticsearch download page here.

As we're installing onto Ubuntu we can use the DEB packages provided:

Listing 3.15: Downloading Elasticsearch

```
$ wget https://download.elasticsearch.org/↵
  elasticsearch/elasticsearch/elasticsearch-1.1.1.↵
  deb
```

Now we install Elasticsearch. We need to tell Elasticsearch where to find our Java JDK installation by setting the JAVA_HOME environment variable. We can then run the dpkg command to install the DEB package.

Listing 3.16: Installing Elasticsearch

```
$ export JAVA_HOME=/usr/lib/jvm/java-7-openjdk-↵
  i386/
$ sudo dpkg -i elasticsearch-1.1.1.deb
```

TIP Remember you can also find tar balls and RPMs for Elasticsearch at http://www.elasticsearch.org/download/.

Installing the package should also automatically start the Elasticsearch server but if it does not then you can manage it via its init script:

Listing 3.17: Starting Elasticsearch

```
$ sudo /etc/init.d/elasticsearch start
```

Introduction to Elasticsearch

Now we've installed Elasticsearch we should learn a little about how it works. A decent understanding is going to be useful later as we use and scale Elasticsearch. Elasticsearch is a text indexing search engine. The best metaphor is the index of a book. You flip to the back of the book[1], look up a word and then find the reference to a page. That means, rather than searching text strings directly, it creates an index from incoming text and performs searches on the index rather than the content. As a result it is very fast.

NOTE This is a simplified explanation. See the site for more information and exposition.

Under the covers Elasticsearch uses Apache Lucene to create this index. Each index is a logical namespace, in Logstash's case the default indexes are named for the day the events are received, for example:

Listing 3.18: A Logstash index

```
logstash-2012.12.31
```

Each Logstash event is made up of fields and these fields become a document inside that index. If we were comparing Elasticsearch to a relational database: an index is a table, a document is a table row and a field is a table column. Like

---

[1]Not the first Puppet book.

a relational database you can define a schema too. Elastic-search calls these schemas "mappings".

NOTE It's important to note that you don't have to specify any mappings for operations, indeed many of searches you'll use with Logstash don't need mappings, but they often makes life much easier. You can see an example of an Elasticsearch mapping at http://untergeek.com/2012/11/05/my-current-templatemapping/. Since Logstash 1.3.2 a default mapping is applied to your Elasticsearch and you generally no longer need to worry about setting your own mapping.

Like a schema, mapping declares what data and data types fields documents contain, any constraints present, unique and primary keys and how to index and search each field. Unlike a schema you can also specify Elasticsearch settings.

You can see the currently applied mapping on your Elastic-search server by using the `curl` command.

Listing 3.19: Showing the current Elasticsearch mapping

```
$ curl localhost:9200/_template/logstash?pretty
```

You can also see mappings applied to specific indexes like so:

Listing 3.20: Showing index-specific mappings

```
$ curl localhost:9200/logstash-2012.12.31/_mapping↵
  ?pretty
```

Indexes are stored in Lucene instances called "shards". There are two types of shards: primary and replica. Primary shards are where your documents are stored. Each new index automatically creates five primary shards. This is a default setting and you can increase or decrease the number of primary shards when the index is created but not AFTER it is created. Once you've created the index the number of primary shards cannot be changed.

Replica shards are copies of the primary shards that exist for two purposes:

- To protect your data.
- To make your searches faster.

Each primary shard will have one replica by default but also have more if required. Unlike primary shards, this can be changed dynamically to scale out or make an index more resilient. Elasticsearch will cleverly distribute these shards across the available nodes and ensure primary and replica shards for an index are not present on the same node.

Shards are stored on Elasticsearch "nodes". Each node is automatically part of an Elasticsearch cluster, even if it's a cluster of one. When new nodes are created they can use unicast or multicast to discover other nodes that share their cluster name and will try to join that cluster. Elasticsearch distributes shards amongst all nodes in the cluster. It can move shards automatically from one node to another in the case of node failure or when new nodes are added.

Configuring our Elasticsearch cluster and node

Next we need to configure our Elasticsearch cluster and node name. Elasticsearch is started with a default cluster name and a random, allegedly amusing, node name, for example "Frank Kafka" or "Spider-Ham". A new random node name is selected each time Elasticsearch is restarted. Remember that new Elasticsearch nodes join any cluster with the same cluster name they have defined. So we want to customize our cluster and node names to ensure we have unique names. To do this we need to edit the /etc/elasticsearch↵ /elasticsearch.yml file. This is Elasticsearch's YAML-based configuration file. Look for the following entries in the file:

Listing 3.21: Initial cluster and node names

```
# cluster.name: elasticsearch
# node.name: "Franz Kafka"
```

We're going to uncomment and change both the cluster and node name. We're going to choose a cluster name of logstash and a node name matching our central server's host name.

Listing 3.22: New cluster and node names

```
cluster.name: logstash
node.name: "smoker"
```

We then need to restart Elasticsearch to reconfigure it.

Listing 3.23: Restarting Elasticsearch

```
$ sudo /etc/init.d/elasticsearch restart
```

We can now check if Elasticsearch is running and active.

Determining Elasticsearch is running

You can tell if Elasticsearch is running by browsing to port 9200 on your host, for example:

Listing 3.24: Checking Elasticsearch is running

```
http://10.0.0.1:9200
```

This should return some status information that looks like:

Listing 3.25: Elasticsearch status information

```
{
  "ok" : true,
  "status" : 200,
  "name" : "smoker",
  "version" : {
    "number" : "0.90.3",
    "snapshot_build" : false
  },
  "tagline" : "You Know, for Search"
}
```

You can also browse to a more detailed status page:

Listing 3.26: Elasticsearch status page

```
http://10.0.0.1:9200/_status?pretty=true
```

This will return a page that contains a variety of information about the state and status of your Elasticsearch server.

TIP You can find more extensive documentation for Elasticsearch at http://www.elasticsearch.org/guide/.

Creating a basic central configuration

Now we've got our environment configured we're going to set up our Logstash configuration file to receive events. We're going to call this file central.conf and create it in the /↵ etc/logstash/conf.d directory.

Listing 3.27: Creating the central.conf file

```
$ sudo touch /etc/logstash/conf.d/central.conf
```

Let's put some initial configuration into the file.

Listing 3.28: Initial central configuration

```
input {
  redis {
    host => "10.0.0.1"
    type => "redis-input"
    data_type => "list"
    key => "logstash"
  }
}
output {
  stdout { }
  elasticsearch {
    cluster => "logstash"
  }
}
```

In our central.conf configuration file we can see the input and output blocks we learned about in Chapter 2. Let's see what each does in this new context.

The central.conf input block

For the input block we've specified one plugin: redis, with four options. The first option, host, specifies which interface that Redis will listen for events on, in our case 10.0.0.1. The second option, type, populates the type field of our event and is used to help identify what events are. The type is only added if the event doesn't already have one specified. If you are adding a type to your events on your remote agent then this is passed through to the central server and the option on the input plugin is ignored.

The data_type option allows you to specify either a list, a channel or a pattern_channel. For lists Redis will use the BLPOP command to process the key, for channels Redis will SUBSCRIBE to the key and for pattern channels Redis will PSUBSCRIBE to the key. The key option specifies the name of a Redis list or channel. For example, as we've specified list as the value of data_type, we've configured a list called logstash.

By configuring this plugin we're telling Logstash to connect to our Redis broker that listens on IP address 10.0.0.1 on port 6379. The broker will be listening for incoming Logstash events in JSON and pass them to a list called logstash↵. When it receives the events Logstash will label them with a type of redis-input.

The central.conf output block

The contents of central.conf's output block is fairly easy to understand. We've already seen the stdout plugin in Chapter 1. Incoming events will be outputted to STDOUT and therefore to Logstash's own log file. I've done this for debugging purposes so we will be more easily able to see our incoming events. In a production environment you would probably disable this to prevent any excess noise being generated.

We've added another plugin called elasticsearch. This plugin sends events from Logstash to Elasticsearch to be stored and made available for searching. The only option we're configuring for this plugin is cluster which tells Logstash the name of the Elasticsearch cluster. Here we've specified `logstash`, which the name of the Elasticsearch cluster we installed earlier. Logstash will attempt to connect to that cluster as a client.

Running Logstash as a service

Now we've provided Logstash with a basic centralized configuration we can start our Logstash process. You can now run the Logstash service.

Listing 3.29: Starting the central Logstash server

```
$ sudo service logstash start
```

You should see a message indicating Logstash is being started.

Checking Logstash is running

We can confirm that Logstash is running by a variety of means. First, we can use the init script itself:

Listing 3.30: Checking the Logstash server is running

```
$ sudo service logstash status
* Logstash Daemon is running.
```

Finally, Logstash will send its own log output to /var/log↵ /logstash/logstash.log. When Logstash starts you should begin to see some informational messages logged to this file, for example:

Listing 3.31: Logstash log output

```
{:message=>"Read config", :level=>:info}
{:message=>"Start thread", :level=>:info}
{:message=>"Registering redis", :identity=>"↵
  default", :level=>:info}
. . .
{:message=>"All plugins are started and registered↵
  .", :level=>:info}
```

Installing Logstash on our first agent

Our central server is now idling waiting to receive events so let's make it happy and set up a Logstash agent to send some of those events to it. We're going to choose one of our CentOS hosts, maurice.example.com with an IP address of 10.0.0.10 as our first agent.

Agent

- Hostname: maurice.example.com
- IP Address: 10.0.0.10

In the agent we're going to begin with sending some Syslog events to the central Logstash server. But first we need to install and configure Logstash on the remote agent. Let's install Logstash now.

First we should download the Yum GPG key.

Listing 3.32: Adding the Yum GPG key

```
$ sudo rpm --import http://packages.elasticsearch.↵
  org/GPG-KEY-elasticsearch
```

We'll now add the Logstash Yum repository to our host. Create a file called /etc/yum.repos.d/logstash.repo and add the following content.

Listing 3.33: Adding the Logstash Yum repository

```
[logstash-1.4]
name=logstash repository for 1.4.x packages
baseurl=http://packages.elasticsearch.org/logstash↵
  /1.4/centos
gpgcheck=1
gpgkey=http://packages.elasticsearch.org/GPG-KEY-↵
  elasticsearch
enabled=1
```

We can then install Logstash via the yum command.

Listing 3.34: Install Logstash via yum

```
$ sudo yum install logstash
```

Our agent configuration

Now we've got our base in place, let's create our agent configuration in /etc/logstash/conf.d. We're going to create a configuration file called `shipper.conf` and then populate it with what we need to begin shipping events.

Listing 3.35: Creating the Logstash agent configuration

```
$ sudo touch /etc/logstash/conf.d/shipper.conf
```

Now let's add our event shipping configuration:

Listing 3.36: Logstash event shipping configuration

```
input {
  file {
    type => "syslog"
    path => ["/var/log/secure", "/var/log/messages↵
    "]
    exclude => ["*.gz"]
  }
}

output {
  stdout { }
  redis {
    host => "10.0.0.1"
    data_type => "list"
    key => "logstash"
  }
}
```

Let's take a look at each block in our configuration file.

The shipper.conf input block

In our remote agent configuration we've specified a single input plugin, `file`. This plugin collects events from files. The `file` plugin is quite clever and does some useful things:

- It automatically detects new files matching our collection criteria.
- It can handle file rotation, for example when you run logrotate.
- It keeps track of where it is up to in a file. Specifically this will load any new events from the point at which Logstash last processed an event. Any new files start from the bottom of the file. See the `sincedb` options of `file` plugin.

To configure the `file` input plugin we've specified a type, `syslog`, to identify events from this input. Then we've specified an array of files to collect events from in the `path` option. In our case we've selected two files containing Syslog output: `/var/log/secure` and `/var/log/messages`. The `path` option also allows us to specify globbing, for example we could collect events from all `*.log` files in the `/var/log/` directory:

Listing 3.37: File input globbing

```
path => [ "/var/log/*.log" ]
```

Or even a recursive glob like:

Listing 3.38: File recursive globbing

```
path => [ "/var/log/**/*log" ]
```

Next, we've used the `exclude` option to specify an array of files from which we specifically do not want to collect events. In our case we've only listed two files in `path` rather than a glob so we don't specifically need to worry about excluding any files. But it's a good idea to put in some basic exclusions as force of habit. So I've specified some useful defaults here: all `*.gz` files. Exclusions are filenames rather than file paths but can include globs like our `*.gz` entry.

TIP You can find more options of the `file` plugin at http://logstash.net/docs/latest/inputs/file.

The shipper.conf output block

Our `output` block contains two plug-ins: `stdout` and `redis`. The `stdout` plugin will send copies of events to the Logstash log file, in this case `/var/log/logstash/logstash.log`. I have this plugin enabled for debugging purposes. In production you may wish to turn it off to avoid generating too much unnecessary noise.

The `redis` plugin is going to send our events from the remote agent to our central Logstash server. We've set three configuration options for the plugin. Firstly, we've told Logstash the `host` to send the events to. In this case our central Logstash server `smoker.example.com` with the IP address of `10.0.0.1`.

WARNING It's important to point out here that Redis has no security controls. The connection between your agent and central server is not encrypted or authenticated. If you care about the security or secrecy of your log events or especially if you don't trust the network over which you're sending this data then you shouldn't use this plugin or you should consider tunneling your traffic through stunnel or a VPN technology.

Do you remember that we specified two options, `data_type` and `key`, in the `redis` input plugin on the central server? On the agent we also need to set these options and their values need to match the values we used on the central server. So we've set `data_type` to `list` and `key` to `logstash`. This allows the output on our remote agent to be matched with the input on our central host.

Installing Logstash as a service

Now we've provided Logstash with a basic centralized configuration we can start our Logstash process. You can now run the Logstash service.

Listing 3.39: Starting the central Logstash server

```
$ sudo service logstash start
Starting Logstash Daemon:  [  OK  ]
```

You should see a message indicating Logstash informing you that Logstash is being started.

Checking Logstash is running

We can confirm that Logstash is running by a variety of means. First, we can use the init script itself:

Listing 3.40: Checking the Logstash server is running

```
$ sudo service logstash status
* Logstash Daemon is running.
```

Finally, Logstash will send its own log output to `/var/log↩/logstash/logstash.log`. When Logstash starts you should begin to see some informational messages logged to this file, for example:

Listing 3.41: Logstash log output

```
{:message=>"Read config", :level=>:info}
{:message=>"Start thread", :level=>:info}
{:message=>"Registering redis", :identity=>"↵
  default", :level=>:info}
. . .
{:message=>"All plugins are started and registered↵
  .", :level=>:info}
```

Sending our first events

We've now got our central server and our first agent set up and configured. We're monitoring the /var/log/secure and the /var/log/messages files and any new events logged to these files should now be passed to the Logstash agent and then sent to the central server. They'll be processed, passed to Elasticsearch, indexed and made available to search.

So how do we send some initial events? One of the files we're monitoring is /var/log/secure which is the destination for security-relevant system logs including log in activity. So let's login to our host via SSH and generate some messages. Before we do though let's watch Logstash's own log files on smoker and maurice.

Listing 3.42: Watching the shipper Logstash logstash.log file

```
maurice$ tail -f /var/log/logstash/logstash.log
```

And:

Listing 3.43: Watching the cental Logstash logstash.log file

```
smoker$ tail -f /var/log/logstash/logstash.log
```

As we have the stdout plugin specified on both hosts we should get a copy of any events generated both log files.

On our central host we could also confirm events are flowing through Redis using the llen command to check the length of the logstash list.

Listing 3.44: Testing Redis is operational

```
$ redis-cli -h 10.0.0.1
redis 10.0.0.1:6379> llen logstash
(integer) 1
```

Now let's generate a specific event by SSH'ing into Maurice.

Listing 3.45: Connecting to Maurice via SSH

```
joker$ ssh root@maurice.example.com
```

NOTE We could also use a tool like logger here to generate some events. We'll see logger again in Chapter 4.

When we check each files we should see events related to our login attempt. Let's look at one of those events:

Listing 3.46: A Logstash login event

```
{
  "message" => "Dec  9 07:53:16 maurice sshd↵
    [31198]: Accepted password for root from ↵
    184.152.74.118 port 55965 ssh2",
  "@timestamp" => "2012-12-09T07:53:16.737Z",
  "@version" => "1",
  "host" => "maurice.example.com",
  "path" => "/var/log/secure",
  "type" => "syslog"
}
```

We can see it is made up of the fields we saw in Chapter 2 plus some additional fields. The host field shows the hostname of the host that generated the event. The path field shows the file /var/log/secure that the event was collected from. Both these fields are specific to the file input plugin that processed this event.

The message gives us the exact message being collected. The @timestamp field provides the date and time of the event. and the @version shows the event schema version. Lastly, the event type of syslog has been added by the file input.

Checking Elasticsearch has received our events

By seeing the events from maurice.example.com in the central server's log files we know the events are flowing. On the central server though one of our outputs is Elasticsearch via the elasticsearch plugin. So we also want to confirm that our events were sent to Elasticsearch, indexed, and are available to search.

We can check this by querying the Elasticsearch server via its HTTP interface. To do this we're going to use the `curl` command.

Listing 3.47: Querying the Elasticsearch server

```
$ curl "http://localhost:9200/_search?q=type:←
  syslog&pretty=true"
{
  "took" : 3,
  "timed_out" : false,
  "_shards" : {
  "total" : 10,
  "successful" : 10,
  "failed" : 0
},
"hits" : {
"total" : 5,
"max_score" : 0.5945348,
"hits" : [ {
  "_index" : "logstash-2013.08.25",
  "_type" : "secure",
  "_id" : "ZSMs-WbdRIqLmszB5w_igw",
  "_score" : 0.5945348, "_source" : {"message":"←
    Aug 25 19:57:55 maurice.example.com sshd←
    [2352]: pam_unix(sshd:session): session opened←
     for user root by (uid=0)","@timestamp":"2013-←
    08-25T19:57:56.118Z","@version":"1","host":"←
    maurice.example.com","path":"/var/log/secure",←
    type":"syslog"}
},
  . . .
```

Here we've issued a GET to the Elasticsearch server running on the localhost on port 9200. We've told it to search all indexes and return all events with `type` of `syslog`. We've also passed `pretty=true` to return our event stream in the more readable 'pretty' format. You can see it's returned some information about how long the query took to process and which indexes were hit. But more importantly it's also returned some events which means our Elasticsearch server is operational and we can search for our events.

NOTE This book used to recommend adding an Elasticsearch mapping template to your Elasticsearch server to customize it for Logstash and to improve performance. Since Logstash 1.3.2 a default template is now automatically applied that takes care of this for you. You can find this default template at https://github.com/logstash/logstash/blob/master/lib/logstash/outpu template.json.

The Logstash Kibana Console

Manually searching for log entries via the Elasticsearch HTTP API seems a little kludgy though. There must be an easier way right? Indeed there is. Built into Logstash is a simple but powerful web interface called Kibana that you can use to query and display your log events. The Kibana web interface is a customizable dashboard that you can extend and modify to suit your environment. It allows the querying of events, creation of tables and graphs as well as sophisticated visualizations.

Since we've already installed Logstash it's just a simple matter of running another variant of the Logstash agent to activate the Kibana web console.

NOTE Remember Logstash's command line flags control what component is run rather than having separate applications for each purpose.

We can start by launching the web interface from the command line using the `logstash` binary:

Listing 3.48: Launching the Logstash Kibana web interface

```
$ /opt/logstash/bin/logstash web
```

You can see that instead of launching the `agent` portion of Logstash we're launching the `web` component.

Once the web interface has started we should be able to browse to the URL, replacing the IP address with one from your environment:

Listing 3.49: Logstash web interface address

```
http://10.0.0.1:9292
```

And then see the interface.

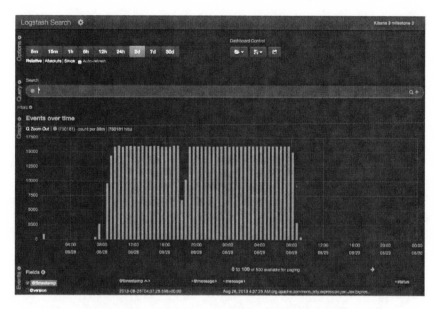

Figure 3.2: The Logstash web interface

This is the default "dark"-themed interface. If you'd prefer there is also a light themed interface you can select by clicking the large cog next to the Logstash Search title.

Figure 3.3: The Logstash web interface's light theme

TIP You can also use the Settings cog to change the base configuration of our dashboard.

By default the Kibana dashboard returns all available events, which you can see from the * in the Query panel. We can instead query for something, for example let's query for all events with a type of syslog.

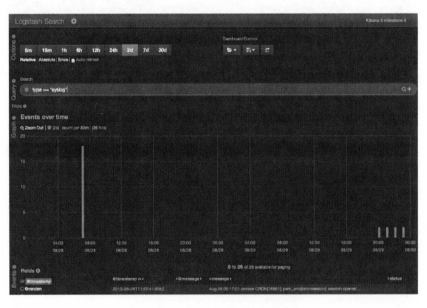

Figure 3.4: Query results

We can then click on specific events to see them in more detail.

Figure 3.5: Specific events

Let's try a more specific query. The Logstash web interface uses the Apache Lucene query syntax to allow you to make queries. The simplest query is just using a simple string, like so:

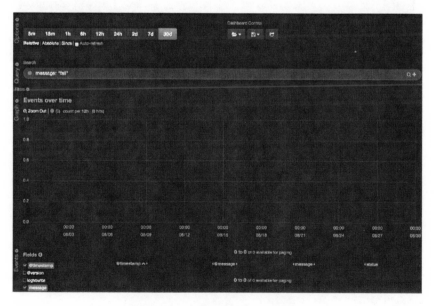

Figure 3.6: Basic query

Here we've searched for the string `fail` and Logstash has returned 0 events which contain the string. Woot! No failures.

We can also perform more sophisticated queries. For example let's search for all events of type apache that contain the string 404 in the message.

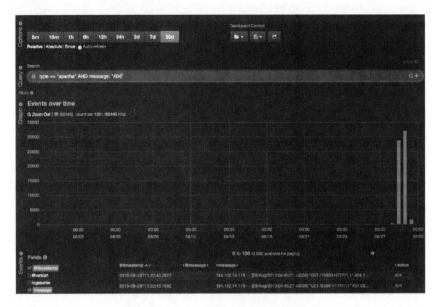

Figure 3.7: Advanced query

You can search any of the fields contained in a Logstash event, for example type, message, etc. You can also use boolean logic like AND, OR and NOT as well as fuzzy and wildcard searches. You can see the full query language in the Apache Lucene documentation.

The dashboard is also highly customizable. You can add, remove or update existing panels by clicking on the edit cog symbol next to a panel.

Figure 3.8: Customizing the dashboard

We can then add, edit or update a variety of different panels.

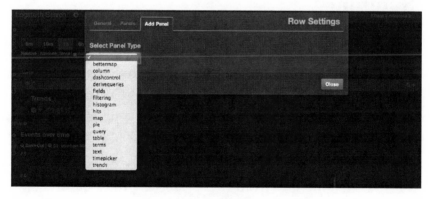

Figure 3.9: Adding a panel

We can then use the Dashboard control panel to save our dashboard, load other dashboards or share a link to this specific dashboard.

Figure 3.10: The Dashboard control panel

This just scratches the surface of what you can do with Kibana. You can build complex queries (including saving them and displaying the results as a new panel), graph and visualize data, produce tables and display data on maps and charts. I recommend you spend some time exploring and customizing Kibana to suit your environment.

Summary

We've made a great start on our log management project. In this chapter we've installed and configured Logstash, Redis and Elasticsearch on a central server. We've installed and configured Logstash on a remote agent and we can easily replicate this configuration (preferably using configuration management tools like Puppet and Chef).

We're collecting logs from two Syslog log files and transmitting them to our central server. We're indexing them and making them searchable via Elasticsearch and the Logstash Kibana interface.

In the next chapter we're going to expand on our implementation and look at processing some additional log sources especially in situations when we can't deploy the Logstash agent.

Chapter 4

Shipping Events without the Logstash agent

Our log management project is going well. We've got some of our Syslog messages centralized and searchable but we've hit a snag. We've discovered some hosts and devices in our environment that can't be managed with the Logstash agent. There are a few different devices that all have varying reasons for not being able to run the agent:

- Small virtual machine with limited memory insufficient to run the agent.
- Some embedded devices and appliances without the ability to install Java and hence run the agent.
- Some outsourced managed hosts where you can't install software of your own.

So to address these hosts we're going to make a slight digression in our project and look at alternatives to running the

Logstash agent and getting events to our central Logstash server.

Using Syslog

The first way we can get our recalcitrant devices to log to Logstash is using a more traditional logging method: Syslog. Instead of using the Logstash agent to send our logs we can enable existing Syslog daemons or services to do it for us.

To do this we're going to configure our central Logstash server to receive Syslog messages and then configure Syslog on the remote hosts to send to it. We're also going to show you how to configure a variety of Syslog services.

A quick introduction to Syslog

Syslog is one of the original standards for computer logging. It was designed by Eric Allman as part of Sendmail and has grown to support logging from a variety of platforms and applications. It has become the default mechanism for logging on Unix and Unix-like systems like Linux and is heavily used by applications running on these platforms as well as printers and networking devices like routers, switches and firewalls.

As a result of its ubiquity on these types of platforms it's a commonly used means to centralize logs from disparate sources. Each message generated by Syslog (and there are variations between platforms) is roughly structured like so:

Listing 4.1: A Syslog message

```
Dec 15 14:29:31 joker systemd-logind[2113]: New ↵
    session 31581 of user bob.
```

They consist of a timestamp, the host that generated the message (here joker), the process and process ID (PID) that generated the message and the content of the message.

Messages also have metadata attached to them in the form of facilities and severities. Messages refer to a facility like:

- AUTH
- KERN
- MAIL
- etcetera

The facility specifies the type of message generated, for example messages from the AUTH facility usually relate to security or authorization, the KERN facility are usually kernel messages or the MAIL facility usually indicates it was generated by a mail subsystem or application. There are a wide variety of facilities including custom facilities, prefixed with LOCAL and a digit: LOCAL0 to LOCAL7, that you can use for your own messages.

Messages also have a severity assigned, for example EMERGENCY, ALERT, and CRITICAL, ranging down to NOTICE, INFO and DEBUG.

TIP You can find more details on Syslog at http://en.wikipedia.org/w

Configuring Logstash for Syslog

Configuring Logstash to receive Syslog messages is really easy. All we need to do is add the `syslog` input plugin to our central server's `/etc/logstash/conf.d/central.conf↩` configuration file. Let's do that now:

Listing 4.2: Adding the `syslog` input

```
input {
  redis {
    host => "10.0.0.1"
    data_type => "list"
    type => "redis-input"
    key => "logstash"
  }
  syslog {
    type => syslog
    port => 5514
  }
}
output {
  stdout { }
  elasticsearch {
    cluster => "logstash"
  }
}
```

You can see that in addition to our `redis` input we've now got `syslog` enabled and we've specified two options:

Listing 4.3: The `syslog` input

```
syslog {
  type => syslog
  port => 5514
}
```

The first option, `type`, tells Logstash to label incoming events as `syslog` to help us to manage, filter and output these events. The second option, `port`, opens port 5514 for both TCP and UDP and listens for Syslog messages. By default most Syslog servers can use either TCP or UDP to send Syslog messages and when being used to centralize Syslog messages they generally listen on port 514. Indeed, if not specified, the `port` option defaults to 514. We've chosen a different port here to separate out Logstash traffic from any existing Syslog traffic flows you might have. Additionally, since we didn't specify an interface (which we could do using the `host` option) the `syslog` plugin will bind to `0.0.0.0` or all interfaces.

TIP You can find the full list of options for the `syslog` input plugin at http://logstash.net/docs/latest/inputs/syslog.

Now, if we restart our Logstash agent, we should have a Syslog listener running on our central server.

Listing 4.4: Restarting the Logstash server

```
$ sudo service logstash restart
```

You should see in your /var/log/logstash/logstash.log↩
 log file some lines indicating the syslog input plugin has
started:

Listing 4.5: Syslog input startup output

```
{:message=>"Starting syslog udp listener", :↩
  address=>"0.0.0.0:5514", :level=>:info}
{:message=>"Starting syslog tcp listener", :↩
  address=>"0.0.0.0:5514", :level=>:info}
```

NOTE To ensure connectivity you will need make sure
any host or intervening network firewalls allow connections
on TCP and UDP between hosts sending Syslog messages and
the central server on port 5514.

Configuring Syslog on remote agents

There are a wide variety of hosts and devices we need to
configure to send Syslog messages to our Logstash central
server. Some will be configurable by simply specifying the
target host and port, for example many appliances or managed devices. In their case we'd specify the hostname or IP
address of our central server and the requisite port number.

Central server

- Hostname: smoker.example.com
- IP Address: 10.0.0.1
- Syslog port: 5514

In other cases our host might require its Syslog daemon or service to be specifically configured. We're going to look at how to configure three of the typically used Syslog daemons to send messages to Logstash:

- RSyslog
- Syslog-NG
- Syslogd

We're not going to go into great detail about how each of these Syslog servers works but rather focus on how to send Syslog messages to Logstash. Nor are we going to secure the connections. The syslog input and the Syslog servers will be receiving and sending messages unencrypted and unauthenticated.

Assuming we've configured all of these Syslog servers our final environment might look something like:

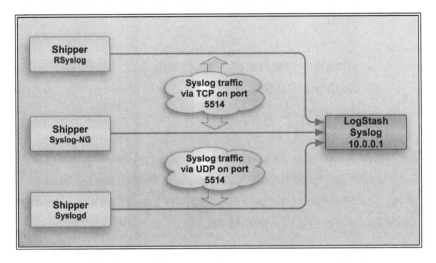

Figure 4.1: Syslog shipping to Logstash

WARNING As I mentioned above Syslog has some variations between platforms. The Logstash `syslog` input plugin supports RFC3164 style syslog with the exception that the date format can either be in the RFC3164 style or in ISO8601. If your Syslog output isn't compliant with RFC3164 then this plugin will probably not work. We'll look at custom filtering in Chapter 5 that may help parse your specific Syslog variant or you can read some further information at http://cookbook.logstash.net/recipes/syslog-pri/.

Configuring RSyslog

The RSyslog daemon has become popular on many distributions, indeed it has become the default Syslog daemon on recent versions of Ubuntu, CentOS, Fedora, Debian, open-SuSE and others. It can process log files, handle local Syslog and comes with an extensible modular plug-in system.

TIP In addition to supporting Syslog output Logstash also supports the RSyslog specific RELP protocol.

We're going to add Syslog message forwarding to our RSyslog configuration file, usually `/etc/rsyslog.conf` (or on some platforms inside the `/etc/rsyslog.d/` directory). To do so we're going to add the following line to the end of our `/↵ etc/rsyslog.conf` file:

Listing 4.6: Configuring RSyslog for Logstash

```
*.* @@smoker.example.com:5514
```

NOTE If you specify the hostname, here `smoker.example.com`, your host will need to be able to resolve it via DNS.

This tells RSyslog to send all messages using `*.*`, which indicates all facilities and priorities. You can specify one or more facilities or priorities if you wish, for example:

Listing 4.7: Specifying RSyslog facilities or priorities

```
mail.* @@smoker.example.com:5514
*.emerg @@joker.example.com:5514
```

The first line would send all `mail` facility messages to our `smoker` host and the second would send all messages of `emerg` priority to the host `joker`.

The `@@` tells RSyslog to use TCP to send the messages. Specifying a single `@` uses UDP as a transport.

TIP I would strongly recommend using the more reliable and resilient TCP protocol to send your Syslog messages.

If we then restart the RSyslog daemon, like so:

Listing 4.8: Restarting RSyslog

```
$ sudo /etc/init.d/rsyslog restart
```

Our host will now be sending all the messages collected by RSyslog to our central Logstash server.

The RSyslog imfile module One of RSyslog's modules provides another method of sending log entries from RSyslog. You can use the imfile module to transmit the contents of files on the host via Syslog. The `imfile` module works much like Logstash's `file` input and supports file rotation and tracks the currently processed entry in the file.

To send a specific file via RSyslog we need to enable the `imfile` module and then specify the file to be processed. Let's update our /etc/rsyslog.conf file (or if your platform supports the /etc/rsyslog.d directory then you can create a file-specific configuration file in that directory).

Listing 4.9: Monitoring files with the imfile module

```
$Modload imfile

$InputFileName "/var/log/apache2/error.log"
$InputFileTag "apache"
$InputFileStateFile "/var/spool/rsyslog/↵
  apache_error_state"
$InputRunFileMonitor
```

The first line, starting with $Modload, loads the `imfile` module. The next lines specify the file be monitored, here /var/log/apache2/error.log, tags these messages in RSyslog with apache and specifies a state file for RSyslog to track the current endpoint processed in the file. Lastly, the $InputRunFileMonitor line initiates file monitoring for this file.

Now, once you've restarted RSyslog, it will be monitoring this file and sending any new lines via Syslog to our Logstash instance (assuming we've configured RSyslog as suggested in the previous section).

TIP You can find the full RSyslog documentation at

http://www.rsyslog.com/.

Configuring Syslog-NG

Whilst largely replaced in modern distributions by RSyslog, there are still a lot of platforms that use Syslog-NG including Gentoo, FreeBSD, Arch Linux and HP UX. Like RSyslog, Syslog-NG is a fully featured Syslog server but its configuration is a bit more substantial than what we needed for RSyslog.

Syslog-NG configuration comes in four types:

- `source` statements - where log messages come from.
- `destination` statements - where to send log messages.
- `filter` statements - how to filter or process log messages.
- `log` statements - actions that combine source, destination and filter statements.

Let's look inside an existing Syslog-NG configuration. Its configuration file is usually `/etc/syslog-ng.conf` or `/etc/⏎ syslog-ng/syslog-ng.conf`. You'll usually find a line something like this inside:

Listing 4.10: Syslog-NG s_src source statement

```
source s_src { unix-dgram("/dev/log"); internal();⏎
  file("/proc/kmsg" program_override("kernel"));
};
```

This basic source statement collects Syslog messages from the host, kernel messages and any internal messages to Syslog-NG. This is usually the default source on most distributions and platforms. If you don't see this source your Syslog-NG server may not be collecting Syslog messages and you should validate its configuration. You may also see additional source statements, for example collecting messages via the network from other hosts.

We then need to define a new destination for our Logstash server. We can do this with a line like so:

Listing 4.11: New Syslog-NG destination

```
destination d_logstash { tcp("10.0.0.1" port(5144)↩
  ); };
```

This tells Syslog-NG to send messages to IP address 10.0.0.1 on port 5144 via TCP. If you have domain name resolution you could instead specify our Logstash server's host name.

Lastly, we will need to specify a log action to combine our source or sources and our destination

Listing 4.12: New Syslog-NG log action

```
log { source(s_src); destination(d_logstash); };
```

This will send all Syslog messages from the s_src source to the d_logstash destination which is our central Logstash server.

To enable the message transmission you'll need to restart

Syslog-NG like so:

Listing 4.13: Restarting Syslog-NG

```
$ sudo /etc/init.d/syslog-ng restart
```

TIP You can find the full Syslog-NG documentation at http://www.balabit.com/sites/default/files/documents/syslog-ng-admin-guide_en.html/index.html.

Configuring Syslogd

The last Syslog variant we're going to look at configuring is the older style Syslogd. While less common it's still frequently seen on older distribution versions and especially in the more traditional Unix platforms.

TIP This includes many of the *BSD-based platforms including OSX.

Configuring Syslogd to send on messages is very simple. Simply find your Syslogd configuration file, usually /etc↩ /syslog.conf and add the following line at the end of the file:

Listing 4.14: Configuring Syslogd for Logstash

```
*.* @smoker.example.com:5514
```

TIP You can find more details about Syslogd configuration at http://linux.die.net/man/5/syslog.conf.

This will send all messages to the host `smoker.example.com` on UDP port 5514. It is important to note that Syslogd generally does not support sending messages via TCP. This may be a problem for you given UDP is a somewhat unreliable protocol: there is absolutely no guarantee that the datagram will be delivered to the destination host when using UDP. Failure rates are typically low but for certain types of data including log events losing them is potentially problematic. You should take this into consideration when using Syslogd and if possible upgrade to a more fully featured Syslog server like Syslog-NG or RSyslog.

Once you've configured the Syslogd you'll need to restart the daemon, for example:

Listing 4.15: Restarting Syslogd

```
$ sudo /etc/init.d/syslogd restart
```

Other Syslog daemons

There are a variety of other Syslog daemons including several for Microsoft Windows. If you need to configure these then please see their documentation.

- Snare for Windows
- KiwiSyslog
- Syslog-Win32
- Cisco devices
- Checkpoint
- Juniper
- F5 BigIP
- HP Jet Direct

WARNING Remember not all of these devices will produce RFC-compliant Syslog output and may not work with the `syslog` input. We'll look at custom filtering in Chapter 5 that may assist in working with your Syslog variant.

Testing with logger

Most Unix and Unix-like platforms come with a handy utility called `logger`. It generates Syslog messages that allow you to easily test if your Syslog configuration is working. You can use it like so:

Listing 4.16: Testing with logger

```
$ logger "This is a syslog message"
```

This will generate a message from the user facility of the priority notice (user.notice) and send it to your Syslog process.

TIP You can see full options to change the facility and priority of logger messages at http://linux.die.net/man/1/logger.

Assuming everything is set up and functioning you should see the resulting log event appear on your Logstash server:

Listing 4.17: Logstash log event from Syslog

```
{
  "host" => "joker.example.com",
  "priority" => 13,
  "timestamp" => "Dec 17 16:00:35",
  "logsource" => "joker.example.com",
  "program" => "bob",
  "pid" => "23262",
  "message" =>"This is a syslog message",
  "severity" => 5,
  "facility" => 1,
  "facility_label" => "user-level",
  "severity_label" => "Notice",
  "@timestamp" => "2012-12-17T16:00:35.000Z",
  "@version => "1",
  "message" => "<13>Dec 17 16:00:35 joker.example.↵
    com bob[23262]: This is a syslog message",
  "type" => "syslog"
}
```

Using the Logstash Forwarder

If you can't use the Logstash agent and Syslog isn't an option then don't despair. We still have plenty of ways to get your logs from your hosts to Logstash. One of those ways is a tool called the Logstash Forwarder (formerly Lumberjack), written by Logstash's author Jordan Sissel.

The Logstash Forwarder (hereafter Forwarder) is designed

to be a lightweight client and server for sending messages to Logstash. It includes a custom-designed protocol and unlike any of our previous transports it also includes some security via SSL encryption of the traffic as well as compression of log traffic. Using the Forwarder you can:

- Follow files (it also respects rename and truncation conditions like log rotation).
- Receive stdin, which is useful for things like piping output to the Forwarder.

So why use the Forwarder at all instead of say Syslog? The Forwarder is designed to be tiny, incredibly memory conservative and very, very fast. None of the existing Syslog servers are really designed to scale and transmit large volumes of events and they often break down at large volumes.

To get it running we're going to configure the Forwarder input plugin on the central Logstash server and then install and configure the Forwarder on a remote host.

Configure the Logstash Forwarder on our central server

The first step in configuring the Forwarder on our central server is to generate a self-signed SSL certificate to secure our log traffic. This is a mandatory step for configuring the Forwarder. You can only send events with the SSL transport enabled and encrypting your traffic.

NOTE You could also use a real certificate if you wished but this is a simpler and faster way to get started.

Create a self-signed SSL certificate

We're going to quickly step through creating the required SSL certificate and key as it is a pretty standard process on most platforms. It requires the openssl binary as a prerequisite.

Listing 4.18: Checking for openssl

```
$ which openssl
/usr/bin/openssl
```

We first generate a private key.

Listing 4.19: Generating a private key

```
$ openssl genrsa -out server.key 2048
Generating RSA private key, 2048 bit long modulus
.......................................+++
....+++
e is 65537 (0x10001)
```

This creates a new file called server.key. This is our SSL certificate key. Don't share it or lose it as it is integral to the security of our solution.

Next we're going to generate a Certificate Signing Request or CSR from which we're going to generate our SSL certificate.

Listing 4.20: Generating a CSR

```
$ openssl req -new -key server.key -batch -out ↵
  server.csr
```

This will generate a file called server.csr which is our sign-ing request.

Lastly we're going to sign our CSR and generate a new cer-tificate.

Listing 4.21: Signing our CSR

```
$ openssl x509 -req -days 3650 -in server.csr -↵
  signkey server.key -out server.crt
Signature ok
subject=/C=AU/ST=Some-State/O=Internet Widgits Pty↵
  Ltd
Getting Private key
```

This will result in a file called server.crt which is our self-signed certificate.

NOTE We've set a very long expiry, 3650 days, for the certificate.

Now let's copy the required files:

- server.key
- server.crt

To our Logstash configuration directory:

Listing 4.22: Copying the key and certificate

```
$ sudo cp server.key server.crt /etc/logstash
```

If you wish to renew the self-signed certificate at some point you'll need to keep the original key and CSR otherwise you can delete the original key and the CSR to keep things tidy.

Listing 4.23: Cleaning up

```
$ rm server.orig.key server.csr
```

Configuring the Lumberjack input

Now we've got our self-signed key we need to add the `lumberjack` input to our central Logstash server's configuration. To do this we're going to edit our /etc/logstash/↩ conf.d/central.conf configuration file.

Listing 4.24: Adding the Lumberjack input

```
input {
  redis {
    host => "10.0.0.1"
    data_type => "list"
    type => "redis-input"
    key => "logstash"
  }
  syslog {
    type => syslog
    port => 5514
  }
  lumberjack {
    port => 6782
    ssl_certificate => "/etc/logstash/server.crt"
    ssl_key => "/etc/logstash/server.key"
    type => "lumberjack"
  }
}
output {
  stdout { }
  elasticsearch {
    cluster => "logstash"
  }
}
```

You can see we've added a new input plugin called
lumberjack:

Listing 4.25: The Lumberjack input

```
lumberjack {
  port => 6782
  ssl_certificate => "/etc/logstash/server.crt"
  ssl_key => "/etc/logstash/server.key"
  type => "lumberjack"
}
```

To configure it we've specified a `port` of 6782. The `lumberjack` input will listen on this TCP port for incoming events. By default the plugin will be bound to all interfaces but you can specify a specific interface with the `host` option.

NOTE You'll need to ensure any firewalls on the host or between the remote client and the central server allow traffic on this port.

We've also specified the certificate and key we created in the last section in the `ssl_certificate` and `ssl_key` options respectively. If we'd put a pass phrase on the key we could specify it here with the `ssl_key_passphrase` option.

Lastly, we've specified a type of `lumberjack` so we can identify events coming in from this input.

TIP You can find the full documentation for the `lumberjack` input at http://logstash.net/docs/latest/inputs/lumber

If we now restart Logstash we will have the `lumberjack` input enabled.

Listing 4.26: Restarting Logstash for Lumberjack

```
$ sudo service logstash restart
```

We can tell if the input plugin has loaded from our /var/↵ log/logstash/logstash.log log file. Check for the following message:

Listing 4.27: Checking Lumberjack has loaded

```
{
  :timestamp => "2013-08-23T04:09:04.426000+0000",
  :message => "Input registered",
  :plugin=><LogStash::Inputs::Lumberjack ↵
    ssl_certificate=>"/etc/logstash/server.crt", ↵
    ssl_key=>"/etc/logstash/server.key", type=>"↵
    lumberjack", charset=>"UTF-8", host=>"0.0.0.0"↵
    >,
  :level=>:info
}
```

The `lumberjack` input is now ready to receive events from our remote clients.

Installing the Logstash Forwarder on the remote host

Now we need to download, compile and install the Forwarder on a remote agent. We're going to choose a new Ubuntu host called gangsteroflove.example.com. As the Forwarder is relatively new software it's not yet packaged in any distributions but it's very easy to create packages from the source and distribute them yourself.

Let's start by downloading the Forwarder from GitHub as a tarball.

Listing 4.28: Downloading the Forwarder

```
$ wget https://github.com/elasticsearch/logstash-↵
  forwarder/archive/master.zip
$ unzip logstash-forwarder-master.zip
$ cd logstash-forwarder-master
```

To compile the Forwarder and create some useful packages we'll need the basic developer tools. On Ubuntu this is achieved by installing the build-essential package alias:

Listing 4.29: Installing the developer tools

```
$ sudo apt-get install build-essential
```

We'll also need to install Go. On Ubuntu we can do this via the Go PPA.

Listing 4.30: Installing Go on Ubuntu

```
$ sudo apt-get install python-software-properties
$ sudo apt-add-repository ppa:duh/golang
$ sudo apt-get update
$ sudo apt-get install golang
```

We'll also need Ruby, Ruby-dev and Rubygems.

Listing 4.31: Installing prerequisite Forwarder packages

```
$ sudo apt-get install ruby rubygems ruby-dev
```

We'll need the `fpm` gem to create the packages.

Listing 4.32: Installing FPM

```
$ sudo gem install fpm
```

Now we can create a DEB package like so:

Listing 4.33: Creating a Forwarder DEB package

```
$ umask 022
$ make deb
```

You'll see a long sequence of compilation and then some final execution as the `fpm` command runs and creates the DEB package.

Listing 4.34: Forwarder make output

```
fpm -s dir -t deb -n logstash-forwarder -v 0.2.0 -↵
  -prefix /opt/logstash-forwarder \
--exclude '*.a' --exclude 'lib/pkgconfig/zlib.pc' ↵
  -C build \
--description "a log shipping tool" \
--url "https://github.com/elasticsearch/logstash-↵
  forwarder" \
bin/logstash-forwarder bin/logstash-forwarder.sh ↵
  lib
Created deb package {"path":"logstash-forwarder_0↵
  .2.0_i386.deb"}
```

We could also run `make rpm` on appropriate RPM-based platforms to build and create RPMs from which to install the Forwarder.

Now let's install our newly created DEB package.

Listing 4.35: Installing the Forwarder

```
$ sudo dpkg -i logstash-forwarder_0.2.0_i386.deb
Selecting previously unselected package logstash-↵
  forwarder.
(Reading database ... 45980 files and directories ↵
  currently installed.)
Unpacking logstash-forwarder (from logstash-↵
  forwarder_0.2.0_i386.deb) ...
Setting up logstash-forwarder (0.2.0) ...
```

From this package the Forwarder will be installed into the

`/opt/logstash-forwarder` directory.

Let's create a configuration directory for the Forwarder.

Listing 4.36: Creating the Forwarder configuration directory

```
$ sudo mkdir /etc/logstash-forwarder
```

We now need to copy our SSL server certificate across to the remote host so we can use it to validate our SSL connection.

Listing 4.37: Copying the Forwarder's SSL certificate

```
smoker$ scp /etc/logstash/server.crt ↵
  bob@gangsteroflove:/etc/logstash-forwarder
```

As I explained either, the Forwarder works by tailing files or taking input from STDIN. We're going to focus on tailing files, which covers most of the logging scenarios you're likely to have.

The Forwarder is configured with a JSON-based configuration file that is specified using the -config command line flag.

Let's create an example of this file now.

Listing 4.38: Creating logstash-forwarder.conf

```
$ touch /etc/logstash-forwarder/logstash-forwarder↵
  .conf
```

Now let's add some configuration to the file.

Listing 4.39: The logstash-forwarder.conf file

```
{
  "network": {
    "servers": [ "10.0.0.1:6782" ],
    "ssl ca": "/etc/logstash-forwarder/server.crt"↵
      ,
    "timeout": 15
  },

  "files": [
{
  "paths": [
    "/var/log/syslog",
    "/var/log/*.log"
  ],
  "fields": { "type": "syslog" }
},
{
  "paths": [
    "/var/log/apache2/*.log"
  ],
  "fields": { "type": "apache" }
}
  ]
}
```

Let's examine the contents of our logstash-forwarder.↵
conf configuration file. It's divided into two JSON stanzas:
network and files.

The network stanza configures the transport portion of the

Forwarder. The first entry `servers` configures the target destination for any Logstash Forwarder log entries, in our case the server at `10.0.0.1` on port 6782 as we configured in our `lumberjack` input above. You can specify an array of servers. The Forwarder will chose one at random and then keep using that server until it becomes unresponsive at which point it will try another server.

We've also defined the location of the SSL server certificate we downloaded from our server. Finally we've specified a server timeout of 15 seconds. This is the time that the Forwarder will wait for a response from a server. If it doesn't receive a response it will select a new server to send to or if no other servers are available it will enter a wait-retry-wait cycle until a server is available.

The next stanza, `files`, controls which files we're monitoring for log events. The `files` stanza is made up of `paths` and optional `fields` blocks. The `paths` blocks specify files or globs of files to watch and receive log entries from. In the case of our example configuration we're monitoring the /↵ var/log/syslog file, all files in /var/log/ ending in *.↵ log and all files in the /var/log/apache2/ directory ending in *.log. You can also see that each `path` block also has a `fields` block. This block will add a `type` field of `syslog` and apache respectively to any log entries from these files.

Now let's run the Forwarder on the command line to test this out.

Listing 4.40: Testing the Forwarder

```
$ /opt/logstash-forwarder/bin/logstash-forwarder -↩
  config /etc/logstash-forwarder/logstash-↩
  forwarder.conf
```

Testing the Logstash Forwarder

Now let's trigger a Syslog message to make sure things are working okay.

Listing 4.41: Test the Forwarder

```
$ logger "This is a message eh?"
```

We should see the connection made on the local client in the Forwarder's STDOUT:

Listing 4.42: The Forwarder connection output

```
2013/08/23 04:18:59 publisher init
2013/08/23 04:18:59.444617 Setting trusted CA from←
    file: /etc/logstash-forwarder/server.crt
2013/08/23 04:18:59.445321 Starting harvester: /←
    var/log/auth.log
. . .
2013/08/23 04:18:59.446050 Starting harvester: /←
    var/log/kern.log
2013/08/23 04:18:59.446459 Starting harvester: /←
    var/log/apache2/access.log
2013/08/23 04:18:59.505609 Connected to localhost←
    :6782
2013/08/23 04:18:59.056065 Registrar received 1 ←
    events
2013/08/23 04:18.59.057591 Saving registrar state.
```

On the central Logstash server we should see a matching event appear in /var/log/logstash/logstash.log:

Listing 4.43: Forwarder events

```
2013-08-23T04:19.00.197Z lumberjack://←
    gangsteroflove.example.com/var/log/syslog: Aug ←
    23 04:19:00 gangsteroflove.example.com root: ←
    This is a message eh?
```

Managing the Logstash Forwarder as a service

Obviously running the Forwarder on the command line isn't a viable option so we're going to implement it as a service. We're going to run the Forwarder using an init script and use an /etc/defaults file to populate the files we'd like to collect events from. On Red Hat-based platforms we could use the /etc/sysconfig approach.

First, grab the Debian-based init script I've made for the Forwarder and the /etc/defaults file that goes with it.

NOTE There is also a Red Hat variant of the init script and an /etc/sysconfig/logstash-forwarder file.

Copy these into place and set executable permissions on the init script:

Listing 4.44: Installing the Forwarder init script

```
$ sudo cp logstash_forwarder_debian.init /etc/init↩
.d/logstash-forwarder
$ sudo chmod 0755 /etc/init.d/logstash-forwarder
$ sudo cp logstash_forwarder_debian.defaults /etc/↩
defaults/logstash-forwarder
```

Let's look inside the /etc/defaults/logstash-forwarder↩ file:

Listing 4.45: The Forwarder defaults file

```
# Options for the Logstash Forwarder
LOGSTASH_FORWARDER_OPTIONS="-config /etc/logstash-↵
  forwarder/logstash-forwarder.conf"
```

Here we're passing in the location of the Forwarder configuration file.

TIP If you were using Puppet or Chef you'd have the Forwarder configuration file as a template and managed to allow you to centrally control the options and files being collected.

If we're happy with these files we can start the Forwarder.

Listing 4.46: Starting the Forwarder

```
$ /etc/init.d/logstash-forwarder start
* logstash-forwarder is not running
* Starting logstash-forwarder
```

We can now confirm the Forwarder is running by checking the PID file, /var/run/logstash-forwarder or by confirming there is a running process:

Listing 4.47: Checking the Forwarder process

```
$ ps -aux | grep 'logstash-forwarder'
root  1501  0.0  0.2  59736  2832 ?SNl  19:51   ↵
  0:00 /opt/logstash-forwarder/bin/logstash-↵
  forwarder -config /etc/logstash-forwarder/↵
  logstash-forwarder.conf
```

We can also send a `logger` event from our remote host that should show up on the central Logstash server.

Other log shippers

If the Logstash Forwarder doesn't suit your purposes there are also several other shippers that might work for you.

Beaver

The Beaver project is another Logstash shipper. Beaver is written in Python and available via PIP.

Listing 4.48: Installing Beaver

```
$ pip install beaver
```

Beaver supports sending events via Redis, STDIN, or zeroMQ. Events are sent in Logstash's `json` codec.

TIP This is an excellent blog post explaining how to get started with Beaver and Logstash.

Woodchuck

Another potential shipping option is a newcomer called Woodchuck. It's designed to be lightweight and is written in Ruby and deployable as a RubyGem. It currently only supports outputting events as Redis (to be received by Logstash's `redis` input) but future plans include ZeroMQ and TCP output support.

Others

- Syslog-shipper
- Remote_syslog
- Message::Passing

Summary

We've now hopefully got some of the recalcitrant hosts into our logging infrastructure via some of the methods we've learnt about in this chapter: Syslog, the Logstash Forwarder or some of the other log shippers. That should put our log management project back on track and we can now look at adding some new log sources to our Logstash infrastructure.

Chapter 5

Filtering Events with Logstash

We've added the hosts that couldn't use the Logstash agent to our Logstash environment. Our project is back on track and we can start to look at some new log sources to get into Logstash. Looking at our project plan we've got four key log sources we need to tackle next:

- Apache server logs
- Postfix server logs
- Java application logs
- A custom log format for an in-house application

Let's look at each type of log source and see how we might go about getting them into Logstash. So far we've put log sources directly into Logstash without manipulating them in any way. It meant we got the message and some small amount of metadata about it (largely its source characteristics) into Logstash. This is a useful exercise. Now all our log data is centralized in one place and we're able to do some basic cross-referencing, querying and analysis.

Our current approach, however, does not add much in the way of context or additional metadata to our events. For example we don't make any use of fields or tags nor did we manipulate or adjust any of the data in any way. And it is this contextual information that makes Logstash and its collection and management of log events truly valuable. The ability to identify, count, measure, correlate and drill down into events to extract their full diagnostic value. To add this context we're going to introduce the concept of filter plugins.

NOTE To save you cutting and pasting we've included an Logstash remote agent configuration file showing all the examples we've used in this chapter at http://logstashbook.com/code/5/shipper.conf.

Apache Logs

The first log source on our list is our Apache web servers. Example.com has a lot of web properties, they are all running on Apache and logging both accesses and errors to log files. Let's start by looking at one of the log events that has been generated:

Listing 5.1: An Apache log event

```
186.4.131.228 - - [20/Dec/2012:20:34:08 -0500] "←
GET /2012/12/new-product/ HTTP/1.0" 200 10902 "←
http://www.example.com/20012/12/new-product/" "←
Mozilla/5.0 (Windows; U; Windows NT 5.1; pl; rv←
:1.9.1.3) Gecko/20090824 Firefox/3.5.3"
```

This entry was produced from Apache's Combined Log Format. You can see there is lots of useful information in this Apache log event:

- A source IP for the client.
- The timestamp.
- The HTTP method, path, and protocol.
- The HTTP response code.
- The size of the object returned to the client.
- The HTTP referrer.
- The User-Agent HTTP request header.

NOTE You can see more details on Apache logging at http://httpd.apache.org/docs/2.4/logs.html.

If we were to send this event to Logstash using our current configuration all of this data would be present in the message field but we'd then need to search for it and it seems like we could do better. Especially given we've got all these useful places to store the appropriate data.

So how do we get the useful data from our Apache log event into Logstash? There are three approaches we could take (and we could also combine one or more of them):

- Filtering events on the agent.
- Filtering events on the central server.
- Sending events from Apache in a better format.

The first two methods would rely on Logstash's `filter` plugins either running locally or on the server. Both have pros and cons. Running locally on the agent reduces the processing load on the central server and ensures only clean, structured events are stored. But you have to maintain a more complex (and preferably managed) configuration locally. On the server side this can be centralized and hopefully easier to manage but at the expense of needing more processing grunt to filter the events.

For this initial log source, we're going to go with the last method, having Apache send custom log output. This is a useful shortcut because Apache allows us to customize logging and we should take advantage of it. By doing this we avoid having to do any filtering or parsing in Logstash and we can concentrate on making best use of the data in Logstash.

Configuring Apache for Custom Logging

To send our log events we're going to use Apache's `LogFormat` and `CustomLog` directives to construct log entries that we can send to Logstash. The `LogFormat` directive allows you to construct custom named log formats and then the `CustomLog` directive uses those formats to write log entries, like so:

Listing 5.2: The Apache LogFormat and CustomLog directives

```
LogFormat "formatoflogevent" nameoflogformat
CustomLog /path/to/logfile nameoflogformat
```

You've probably used the `CustomLog` directive before, for example to enable logging for a virtual host, like so:

Listing 5.3: Apache VirtualHost logging configuration

```
<VirtualHost *:80>
  DocumentRoot /var/www/html/vhost1
  ServerName vhost1.example.com

  <Directory "/var/www/html/vhost1">
Options FollowSymLinks
AllowOverride All
  </Directory>

  CustomLog /var/log/httpd/vhost1.access combined

</VirtualHost>
```

In this example we're specifying the `combined` log format which refers to the default Combined Log Format that generated the event we saw earlier.

NOTE The Combined Log Format is an extension of another default format, the Common Log Format, with the added fields of the HTTP referrer and the User-Agent.

The `LogFormat` directive for Apache's Combined Log Format would be (and you should be able to find this line in your Apache configuration files):

Listing 5.4: The Apache Common Log Format LogFormat directive

```
LogFormat "%h %l %u %t \"%r\" %>s %b \"%{Referer}i↩
  \" \"%{User-agent}i\"" combined
```

NOTE And yes `referer` is spelt incorrectly.

Each log format is constructed using % directives combined with other text. Each % directive represents some piece of data, for example %h is the IP address of the client connecting to your web server and %t is the time of the access request.

TIP You can find a full list of the % directives at http://httpd.apache.org/docs/2.4/mod/mod_log_config.html#formats.

As Apache's log output is entirely customizable using these % directives we can write our log entries in any format we want including, conveniently, constructing structured data events. To take advantage of this we're going to use Apache's LogFormat directive to construct a JSON hash replicating Logstash's json codec. This will allow us to take advantage of the % directives available to add some context to our events.

Creating a Logstash log format

To create a custom log format we need to add our new LogFormat directive to our Apache configuration. To do this we are going to create a file called apache_log.conf and add it to our Apache conf.d directory, for example on Red Hat-based systems we'd add it to /etc/httpd/conf.d/ and on Debian-based systems to /etc/apache2/conf.d. Populate the file with the following LogFormat directive:

Listing 5.5: Apache custom JSON LogFormat

```
LogFormat "{ \
  \"host\":\"host.example.com\", \
  \"path\":\"/var/log/httpd/logstash_access_log\",↵
   \
  \"tags\":[\"wordpress\",\"www.example.com\"], \
  \"message\": \"%h %l %u %t \\\"%r\\\" %>s %b\", ↵
   \
  \"timestamp\": \"%{%Y-%m-%dT%H:%M:%S%z}t\", \
  \"useragent\": \"%{User-agent}i\", \
  \"clientip\": \"%a\", \
  \"duration\": %D, \
  \"status\": %>s, \
  \"request\": \"%U%q\", \
  \"urlpath\": \"%U\", \
  \"urlquery\": \"%q\", \
  \"method\": \"%m\", \
  \"bytes\": %B, \
  \"vhost\": \"%v\" \
}" logstash_apache_json
```

NOTE To save you cutting and pasting this we've included
an example file at http://logstashbook.com/code/5/apache_-
log.conf. You should edit the various sections to add your
own hosts, source info and tags.

This rather complex looking arrangement produces Apache
log data as a JSON hash. One of the reasons it looks so com-

plex is that we're escaping the quotation marks and putting in backslashes to make it all one line and valid JSON. We're specifying the host and path manually and you could use any values that suited your environment here. We're also manually specifying an array of tags in the tags field, here identifying that this is a Wordpress site and it is the www↵.example.com page. You would update these fields to suit your environment.

TIP To manage the LogFormat better I recommend managing the log.conf file as a Puppet or Chef template. That would allow you to centrally control values like the `host`, `path` and `tags` field on a host.

The message field contains the standard Common Log Format event that is generated by Apache. This is useful if you have other tools that consume Apache logs for which you still want the default log output.

The remaining items specified are fields and contain the core of the additional context we've added to our Apache log events. It breaks out a number of the elements of the Common Log Format into their own fields and adds a couple more items, such as vhost via the %v directive. You can easily add additional fields from the available directives if required. Remember to ensure that the field is appropriately escaped if it is required.

TIP As a reminder, you can find a full list of the %

directives at http://httpd.apache.org/docs/2.4/mod/mod_-log_config.html#formats.

Let's add the `CustomLog` directive to our `apache_log.conf` file to actually initiate the logging:

Listing 5.6: Adding the CustomLog directive

```
CustomLog /var/log/httpd/logstash_access_log ↵
  logstash_apache_json
```

And now restart Apache to make our new configuration active.

Listing 5.7: Restarting Apache

```
$ sudo /etc/init.d/httpd restart
```

This will result in Apache creating a log file, `/var/log/↵httpd/logstash_access_log`, that will contain our new log entries.

TIP Remember to add this file to your normal log rotation and you may want to consider turning off your existing Apache logging rather than writing duplicate log entries and wasting Disk I/O and storage. You could alternatively increase the tempo of your log rotation and keep short-term logs as backups and remove them more frequently.

Let's take a look at one of those entries now:

Listing 5.8: A JSON format event from Apache

```
{
  "host" => "maurice.example.com"
  "path" => "/var/log/httpd/logstash_access_log",
  "tags" => [
    [0] "wordpress",
    [1] "www.example.com"
  ],
  "message" => "10.0.0.1 - - [25/Aug/2013:21:22:52↩
    +0000] \"GET / HTTP/1.1\" 304 -",
  "timestamp" => "2013-08-25T21:22:52+0000",
  "clientip" => "10.0.0.1",
  "duration" => 11759,
  "status" => 304,
  "request" => "/index.html",
  "urlpath" => "/index.html",
  "urlquery" => "",
  "method" => "GET",
  "bytes" => 0,
  "vhost" => "10.0.0.1",
  "@timestamp" => "2013-08-25T21:22:53.261Z",
  "@version" => "1",
  "type" => "apache"
}
```

TIP You can also output JSON events from Syslog using RSyslog as you can learn at http://untergeek.com/2012/10/11/usi

rsyslog-to-send-pre-formatted-json-to-logstash/. You can also achieve the same results from recent versions of the Squid proxy which has added a LogFormat capability. Similarly with Nginx.

Sending Apache events to Logstash

So how do we get those log entries from our host to Logstash? There are a number of potential ways we discovered in Chapters 3 and 4 to input the events. We could use the `file` input plugin to input the events from Apache.

Listing 5.9: Apache logs via the file input

```
file {
  type => "apache"
  path => ["/var/log/httpd/logstash_access_log"]
  codec => "json"
}
```

And then use an `output` plugin like the `redis` plugin we used in Chapter 3. Or we could use a tool like the Logstash Forwarder (formerly Lumberjack) (introduced in Chapter 4) and specify our `/var/log/httpd/logstash_access_log` file as one its inputs.

Note that in order for our inputs to receive our new events we need to specify the codec they are in. We do this by adding the `codec` option to the plugin configuration like so:

Listing 5.10: Apache events via the Logstash Forwarder

```
lumberjack {
  port => 6782
  ssl_certificate => "/etc/logstash/server.crt"
  ssl_key => "/etc/logstash/server.key"
  codec => "json"
  type => "lumberjack"
}
```

The codec option tells Logstash that the incoming events are in the json codec. If the events are not in that format it will fall back to the plain codec in which Logstash assumes incoming events are plain strings and parses them as such.

Once you've configured your agent and central server to receive your Apache logs and restarted the required services you should see Apache log events flowing through to ElasticSearch. Let's look at one of these events in the Logstash Kibana interface:

Figure 5.1: Apache log event

We can see that the various pieces of context we've added are now available as tags and fields in the Logstash Kibana interface. This allows us to perform much more sophisticated and intelligent queries on our events. For example, I'd like to see all the events that returned a 404 status code. I can now easily query this using the field named status:

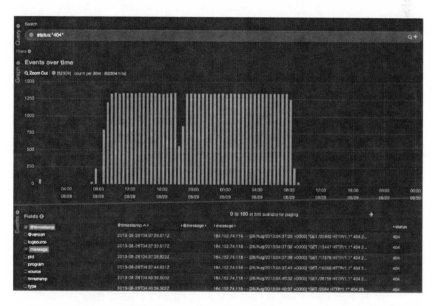

Figure 5.2: Querying for 404 status codes

We can also combine these fields to drill down in more precise queries, for example selecting specific virtual hosts and querying for status codes, specific requests and methods.

TIP We could also use filters, as we'll see shortly, to extract more data from our log entries. For example we could use the useragent or geoip filters to add user agent and GeoIP data respectively.

We can also now quickly and easily drill down into our log data to find events we care about or that are important when troubleshooting.

TIP We'll also see how these more contextual events can be output as alerts or gathered together to produce useful metrics in Chapter 6.

Postfix Logs

Now our Apache logs are pouring into Logstash we need to move onto our next target: Postfix mail server logs. Unfortunately, unlike Apache logs, we can't customize the Postfix log output. We're going to need to use our first `filter` plugins to parse the Postfix events to make them more useful to us. Let's start by looking at a Postfix log entry:

Listing 5.11: A Postfix log entry

```
Dec 24 17:01:03 localhost postfix/smtp[20511]: ↵
  F31B56FF99: to=<james@lovedthanlost.net>, relay=↵
  aspmx.l.google.com[2607:f8b0:400e:c01::1b]:25, ↵
  delay=1.2, delays=0.01/0.01/0.39/0.84, dsn↵
  =2.0.0, status=sent (250 2.0.0 OK 1356368463 ↵
  np6si20817603pbc.299)
```

This log entry is for a sent email and there's quite a lot going on in it with plenty of potential information that we might want to use. Adding it to Logstash in its current form, however, will result in all this information being pushed into the message field as we can see here with a similar event:

Listing 5.12: Unfiltered Postfix event

```
{
  "message" => "Aug 31 01:18:55 smoker postfix/↵
    smtp[25873]: 2B238121203: to=<james@example.↵
    com>, relay=aspmx.l.google.com↵
    [74.125.129.27]:25, delay=3.5, delays↵
    =0.05/0.01/0.47/3, dsn=2.0.0, status=sent (250↵
     2.0.0 OK 1377911935 tp5si709880pac.251 - ↵
    gsmtp)",
  "@timestamp" => "2013-08-31T01:29:42.416Z",
  "@version" => "1",
  "type" => "postfix",
  "host" => "smoker.example.com",
  "path" => "/var/log/mail.log"
}
```

Yep, that's not particularly helpful to us so let's do some basic filtering with Logstash to extract some of that useful information.

Our first filter

For our Postfix logs we're going to do our filtering on the remote agent host so we're sending clean json codec logs to the central Logstash server. To do this we're going to introduce our first filter plugin: grok. The grok filter plugin parses arbitrary text and structures it. It does this using patterns which are packaged regular expressions. As not everyone is a regular expression ninja[1] Logstash ships with a large collection: 120 patterns at the time of writing - of pre-existing patterns that you can use. If needed, it is also very easy to write your own.

NOTE You can find the full list of built-in patterns in Logstash at https://github.com/logstash/logstash/tree/master/patter

---

Firstly, let's collect our Postfix log entries. We're going to use our smoker.example.com host which runs Ubuntu and the Logstash agent so we can add a file input plugin like so to our shipper.conf:

Listing 5.13: File input for Postfix logs

```
input {
  file {
    type => "postfix"
    path => ["/var/log/mail.*"]
  }
}
```

Here we're grabbing all log files from the /var/log directory that match the glob: mail.*.

Now let's add a grok filter to filter these incoming events:

---

[1]And stop calling people 'ninjas' anyway everyone.

Listing 5.14: Postfix grok filter

```
filter {
  if [type] == "postfix" {
    grok {
      match => [ "message", "%{SYSLOGBASE}" ]
      add_tag => [ "postfix", "grokked" ]
    }
  }
}
```

We've added a `grok` filter to our `filter` block. We've first specified a conditional that matches the `type` with a value of `postfix`. This is really important to our filtering process because a filter should generally only match those events for which it's relevant. So in our case only those events with a type of `postfix` will be processed by this filter. All other events will ignore the filter and move on.

NOTE You can see a full list of the `grok` filter's options at http://www.logstash.net/docs/latest/filters/grok.

We've next specified the `match` option which does the hard work of actually "grokking" our log event:

Listing 5.15: The grok pattern for Postfix logs

```
match => [ "message", "%{SYSLOGBASE}" ]
```

Patterns are designed to match and extract specific data from your logs to create data structures from unstructured log strings. They are constructed of regular expressions and structured like so:

Listing 5.16: The syntax and the semantic

```
%{syntax:semantic}
```

The `syntax` is the name of the pattern, for example SYSLOGBASE, being used in the match. The `semantic` is optional and is an identifier for any data matched by the pattern (think of it like assigning a value to a variable).

For our pattern we've used one of Logstash's built-in patterns: SYSLOGBASE. Let's look at the content of this pattern which we can find at https://github.com/logstash/logstash/blob/master/patterns/grok-patterns:

Listing 5.17: The SYSLOGBASE pattern

```
SYSLOGBASE %{SYSLOGTIMESTAMP:timestamp} (?:%{↵
  SYSLOGFACILITY} )?%{SYSLOGHOST:logsource} %{↵
  SYSLOGPROG}:
```

NOTE Again you can find the full list of built-in patterns in Logstash at https://github.com/logstash/logstash/tree/master/patter

---

Each pattern starts with a name, which is the `syntax` we saw above. It is then constructed of either other patterns or regular expressions. If we drill down into the patterns that make up SYSLOGBASE we'll find regular expressions at their core. Let's look at one of the patterns in SYSLOGBASE:

Listing 5.18: The SYSLOGPROG pattern

```
SYSLOGPROG %{PROG:program}(?:\[%{POSINT:pid}\])?
```

More patterns! We can see the SYSLOGPROG pattern is made up of two new patterns: PROG which will save any match as program and POSINT which will save any match as pid. Let's see if we can drill down further in the PROG pattern:

Listing 5.19: The PROG pattern

```
PROG (?:[\w._/%-]+)
```

Ah ha! This new pattern is an actual regular expression. It matches the Syslog program, in our event the postfix⏎/smtp, portion of the log entry. This, combined with the POSINT pattern, will match the program and the process ID from our event and save them both as program and pid respectively.

So what happens when a match is made for the whole SYSLOGBASE pattern? Let's look at the very start of our Postfix log event.

Listing 5.20: Postfix date matching

```
Aug 31 01:18:55 smoker postfix/smtp[25873]:
```

Logstash will apply the pattern to this event. First matching the date portion of our event with the SYSLOGTIMESTAMP↵ pattern and saving the value of that match to timestamp. It will then try to match the SYSLOGFACILITY, SYSLOGHOST and SYSLOGPROG patterns and, if successful, save the value of each match too.

So now these have matched what's next? We know Logstash has managed to match some data and saved that data. What does it now do with that data? Logstash will take each match and create a field named for the semantic, for example in our current event timestamp, program and pid would all become fields added to the event.

The semantic field will be saved as a string by default. If you wanted to change the field type, for example if you wish to use the data for a calculation, you can add a suffix to the pattern to do so. For example to save a semantic as an integer we would use:

Listing 5.21: Converting semantic data

```
%{POSINT:PID:int}
```

Currently the only supported conversions are int for converting to integers and float for converting to a float.

Let's see what happens when the SYSLOGBASE pattern is used to grok our Postfix event. What fields does our event contain?

Listing 5.22: The Postfix event's fields

```
{
    . . .
    "timestamp"=> "Aug 31 01:18:55",
    "logsource"=> "smoker",
    "pid"=> "25873",
    "program"=> "postfix/smtp",
    . . .
}
```

NOTE If you don't specify a semantic then a corresponding field will not be automatically created. See the named_-captures_only option for more information.

Now instead of an unstructured line of text we have a structured set of fields that contain useful data from the event that we can use.

Now let's see our whole Postfix event after it has been grokked:

Listing 5.23: A fully grokked Postfix event

```
{
  "host" => "smoker.example.com",
  "path" => "/var/log/mail.log",
  "tags" => ["postfix", "grokked"],
  "timestamp" => "Aug 31 01:18:55",
  "logsource" => "smoker",
  "pid" => "25873",
  "program" => "postfix/smtp",
  "@timestamp" => "2013-08-31T01:18:55.831Z",
  "@version" => "1",
  "message" => "Aug 31 01:18:55 smoker postfix/↵
    smtp[25873]: 2B238121203: to=<james@example.↵
    com>, relay=aspmx.l.google.com↵
    [74.125.129.27]:25, delay=3.5, delays↵
    =0.05/0.01/0.47/3, dsn=2.0.0, status=sent (250↵
     2.0.0 OK 1377911935 tp5si709880pac.251 - ↵
    gsmtp)",
  "type" => "postfix"
}
```

Our grokked event also shows the result of another option we've used in the grok filter: add_tag. You see the tags field now has two tags in it: postfix and grokked.

TIP You can remove tags from events using the remove_-tag option.

Now we've seen a very basic example of how to do filtering with Logstash. What if we want to do some more sophisticated filtering using filters we've written ourselves?

Adding our own filters

So now we've got some data from our Postfix log event but there is a lot more useful material we can get out. So let's start with some information we often want from our Postfix logs: the Postfix component that generated it, the Process ID and the Queue ID. All this information is contained in the following segment of our Postfix log event:

Listing 5.24: Partial Postfix event

```
postfix/smtp[25873]: 2B238121203:
```

So how might we go about grabbing this information? Well, we've had a look at the existing patterns Logstash provides and they aren't quite right for what we need so we're going to add some of our own.

There are two ways to specify new patterns:

- Specifying new external patterns from a file, or
- Using the named capture regular expression syntax.

Let's look at external patterns first.

Adding external patterns

We add our own external patterns from a file. Let's start by creating a directory to hold our new Logstash patterns:

Listing 5.25: Creating the patterns directory

```
$ sudo mkdir /etc/logstash/patterns
```

Now let's create some new patterns and put them in a file called /etc/logstash/patterns/postfix. Here are our new patterns:

Listing 5.26: Creating new patterns

```
COMP ([\w._\/%-]+)
COMPID postfix\/%{COMP:component}(?:\[%{POSINT:pid↵
  }\])?
QUEUEID ([0-9A-F]{,11})
POSTFIX %{SYSLOGTIMESTAMP:timestamp} %{SYSLOGHOST:↵
  hostname} %{COMPID}: %{QUEUEID:queueid}
```

Each pattern is relatively simple and each pattern builds upon the previous patterns. The first pattern COMP grabs the respective Postfix component, for example smtp, smtpd or qmgr. We then use this pattern inside our COMPID pattern. In the COMPID pattern we also use one of Logstash's built-in patterns POSINT or "positive integer," which matches on any positive integers, to return the process ID of the event. Next we have the QUEUEID pattern which matches the Postfix queue ID, which is an up to 11 digit hexadecimal value.

TIP If you write a lot of Ruby regular expressions you may find Rubular really useful for testing them.

Lastly, we combine all the previous patterns in a new pattern called POSTFIX.

Now let's use our new external patterns in the grok filter.

Listing 5.27: Adding new patterns to grok filter

```
if [type] == "postfix" {
  grok {
    patterns_dir => ["/etc/logstash/patterns"]
    match => [ "message", "%{POSTFIX}" ]
    add_tag => [ "postfix", "grokked"]
  }
}
```

You can see we've added the patterns_dir option which tells Logstash to look in that directory and load all the patterns it finds in there. We've also specified our new pattern, POSTFIX, which will match all of the patterns we've just created. Let's look at our Postfix event we've parsed with our new pattern.

Listing 5.28: Postfix event grokked with external patterns

```
{
  "host" => "smoker.example.com",
  "path" => "/var/log/mail.log",
  "tags" => ["postfix", "grokked"],
  "timestamp" => "Aug 31 01:18:55",
  "hostname" => "smoker",
  "component" => "smtp",
  "pid" => "25873",
  "queueid" => "2B238121203",
  "@timestamp" => "2013-08-31T01:18:55.361Z",
  "@version" => "1",
  "message" => "Aug 31 01:18:55 smoker postfix/↵
    smtp[25873]: 2B238121203: to=<james@example.↵
    com>, relay=aspmx.l.google.com↵
    [74.125.129.27]:25, delay=3.5, delays↵
    =0.05/0.01/0.47/3, dsn=2.0.0, status=sent (250↵
      2.0.0 OK 1377911935 tp5si709880pac.251 - ↵
    gsmtp)",
  "type" => "postfix"
}
```

We can see we've got new fields in the event: component, and queueid.

Using named capture to add patterns

Now let's look at the named capture syntax. It allows you to specify pattern inline rather than placing them in an external file. Let's take an example using our pattern for matching the

Postfix queue ID.

Listing 5.29: A named capture for Postfix's queue ID

```
(?<queueid>[0-9A-F]{,11})
```

The named capture looks like a regular expression, prefixed with the name of the field we'd like to create from this match. Here we're using the regular expression [0-9A-F]{,11} to match our queue ID and then storing that match in a field called queueid.

Let's see how this syntax would look in our grok filter replacing all our external patterns with named captures.

Listing 5.30: Adding new named captures to the grok filter

```
if [type] == "postfix" {
  grok {
    match => [ "message", "%{SYSLOGTIMESTAMP:↵
    timestamp} %{SYSLOGHOST:hostname} postfix↵
    \/(?<component>[\w._\/%-]+)(?:\[%{POSINT:pid↵
    }\]): (?<queueid>[0-9A-F]{,11})" ]
    add_tag => [ "postfix", "grokked"]
  }
}
```

We've used three built-in patterns and our new named capture syntax to create two new patterns: component and queueid. When executed, this grok filter would create the same fields as our external patterns did:

Listing 5.31: Postfix event filtered with named captures

```
{

  . . .

  "timestamp"=> "Aug 31 01:18:55",
  "hostname"=> "smoker",
  "component"=> "smtp",
  "pid"=> "25873",
  "queueid"=> "2B238121203"

  . . .

}
```

TIP If your pattern fails to match an event then Logstash will add the tag _grokparsefailure to the event. This indicates that your event was tried against the filter but failed to parse. There are two things to think about if this occurs. Firstly, should the event have been processed by the filter? Check that the event is one you wish to grok and if not ensure the correct type, tags or field matching is set. Secondly, if the event is supposed to be grokked, test your pattern is working correctly using a tool like the GrokDebugger written by Nick Ethier or the grok binary that ships with the Grok application.

Extracting from different events

We've now extracted some useful information from our Postfix log event but looking at some of the other events Postfix generates there's a lot more we could extract. Thus far
we've extracted all of the common information Postfix events
share: date, component, queue ID, etc. But Postfix events
each contain different pieces of data that we're not going to
be able to match with just our current pattern. Compare
these two events:

Listing 5.32: Postfix event

```
Dec 26 10:45:01 localhost postfix/pickup[27869]: ↵
  841D26FFA8: uid=0 from=<root>
Dec 26 10:45:01 localhost postfix/qmgr[27370]: 841↵
  D26FFA8: from=<root@smoker>, size=336, nrcpt=1 (↵
  queue active)
```

They both share the initial items we've matched but have
differing remaining content. In order to match both these
events we're going to adjust our approach a little and use
multiple grok filters. To do this we're going to use one of
the pieces of data we have already: the Postfix component.
Let's start by adjusting the grok filter slightly:

Listing 5.33: Updated grok filter

```
if [type] == "postfix" {
  grok {
    patterns_dir => ["/etc/logstash/patterns"]
    match => [ "message", "%{POSTFIX}" ]
    add_tag => [ "postfix", "grokked", "%{[↵
      component]}" ]
  }
}
```

You'll note we've added an additional tag, %{[component]}. This syntax allows us to add the value of any field as a tag. In this case if the two log lines we've just seen were processed then they'd result in events tagged with:

Listing 5.34: Postfix component tagged events

```
"tags"=> [ "postfix", "grokked", "pickup" ]
"tags"=> [ "postfix", "grokked", "qmgr" ]
```

Logstash calls this %{field} syntax its sprintf format. This format allows you to refer to field values from within other strings.

TIP You can find full details on this syntax at http://www.logstash.n

---

You can also refer to nested fields using this syntax, for example:

Listing 5.35: Nested field syntax

```
{
  "component" => {
    "pid" => "12345"
    "queueid" => "ABCDEF123456"
  }
}
```

If we wanted to refer to the pid in this nested event we would use, %{[component][pid]}.

TIP For top-level fields you can omit the surrounding square brackets if you wish, for example %component.

Next we're going to add a new grok filter to process a specific Postfix component in our case qmgr:

Listing 5.36: A grok filter for qmgr events

```
grok {
  tags => "qmgr"
  patterns_dir => ["/etc/logstash/patterns"]
  match=> [ "message", "%{POSTFIXQMGR}" ]
}
```

This matches any event tagged with qmgr and matches the message against the POSTFIXQMGR pattern. Let's look at our

/etc/logstash/patterns/postfix file now:

Listing 5.37: The /etc/logstash/patterns/postfix file

```
COMP ([\w._\/%-]+)
COMPPID postfix\/%{COMP:component}(?:\[%{POSINT:↵
  pid}\])?
QUEUEID ([A-F0-9]{5,15}{1})
EMAILADDRESSPART [a-zA-Z0-9_.+-=:]+
EMAILADDRESS %{EMAILADDRESSPART:local}@%{↵
  EMAILADDRESSPART:remote}
POSTFIX %{SYSLOGTIMESTAMP:timestamp} %{SYSLOGHOST:↵
  hostname} %{COMPPID}: %{QUEUEID:queueid}
POSTFIXQMGR %{POSTFIX}: (?:removed|from=<(?:%{↵
  EMAILADDRESS:from})?>(?:, size=%{POSINT:size}, ↵
  nrcpt=%{POSINT:nrcpt} \(%{GREEDYDATA:queuestatus↵
  }\))?)
```

You can see we've added some new patterns to match email addresses and our POSTFIXQMGR pattern to match our qmgr log event. The POSTFIXQMGR pattern uses our existing POSTFIX↵ pattern plus adds patterns for the fields we expect in this log event. The tags field and remaining fields of the resulting event will look like:

Listing 5.38: A partial filtered Postfix event

```
{
    . . .
    "tags" => ["postfix", "grokked", "qmgr"],
    "timestamp" => "Dec 26 20:25:01",
    "hostname" => "localhost",
    "component" => "qmgr",
    "pid" => "27370",
    "queueid" => "D1BDA6FFA8",
    "from" => "root@smoker",
    "local" => "root",
    "remote" => "smoker",
    "size" => "336",
    "nrcpt" => "1",
    "queuestatus" => "queue active"
    . . .
}
```

You can see we've now got all of the useful portions of our event neatly stored in fields that we can query and work with. From here we can easily add other grok filters to process the other types of Postfix events and parse their data.

Setting the timestamp

We've extracted much of the information contained in our Postfix log event but you might have noticed one thing: the timestamp. You'll notice we're extracting a timestamp from our event using the SYSLOGTIMESTAMP pattern which matches data like Dec 24 17:01:03 and storing it as a field called timestamp. But you'll also note that each event also has a @timestamp value and that they are often not the same! So what's happening here? The first timestamp is when the event actually occurred on our host and the second @timestamp is when Logstash first processed the event. We clearly want to ensure we use the first timestamp to ensure we know when events occurred on our hosts.

We can, however, reconcile this difference using another filter plugin called date. Let's add it to our configuration after the grok filter.

Listing 5.39: The date filter

```
if [type] == "postfix" {
  grok {
    patterns_dir => ["/etc/logstash/patterns"]
    match => [ "message", "%{POSTFIX}" ]
    add_tag => [ "postfix", "grokked"]
  }
  date {
    match => [ "timestamp", "MMM dd HH:mm:ss", "↵
      MMM  d HH:mm:ss" ]
    add_tag => [ "dated" ]
  }
}
```

We can see our new date filter. We've specified the match option with the name of the field from which we want to create our time stamp: the timestamp field we created in the grok filter. To allow Logstash to parse this timestamp we're also specifying the date format of the field. In our case we've matched against two date formats: `MMM dd ↵ HH:mm:ss` and `MMM d HH:mm:ss`. These two formats cover the standard Syslog log format and will match our incoming data, `Dec 24 17:01:03`. The date matching uses Java's Joda-Time library and you can see the full list of possible values at `http://docs.oracle.com/javase/7/docs/api/java/text/SimpleDateFormat.html`.

When the `date` filter runs it will replace the contents of the existing `@timestamp` field with the contents of the `timestamp` field we've extracted from our event.

NOTE You can see a full list of the `date` filter's options at http://www.logstash.net/docs/latest/filters/date.

We're also adding a tag `dated` to the event. You'll note we keep adding tags to events as they are filtered. I find this a convenient way to track what filtering or changes have occurred to my event. I can then tell at a glance which events have been changed and what has been done to them.

After performing this filtering, we can see that the timestamps on our events are now in sync and correct.

Listing 5.40: Postfix event timestamps

```
{
  . . .
  "timestamp" => "Dec 24 17:01:03",
  "@timestamp" =>"2012-12-24T17:01:03.000Z",
  . . .
}
```

Before we move on let's visually examine what Logstash's workflow is for our Postfix events:

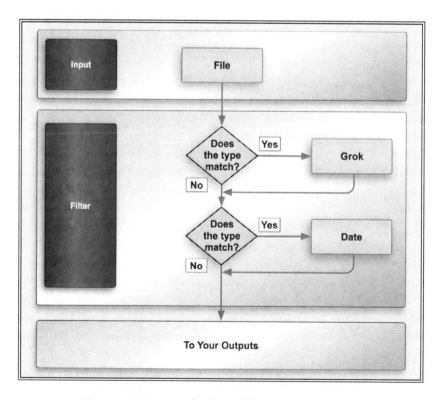

Figure 5.3: Postfix log filtering workflow

With this final piece our Postfix logs are now largely under control and we can move onto our final log source.

Filtering Java application logs

We've got one last data source we need to look at in this chapter: our Java application logs. We're going to start with our Tomcat servers. Let's start with inputting our Tomcat events which we're going to do via the `file` input plugin..

Listing 5.41: File input for Tomcat logs

```
file {
  type => "tomcat"
  path => ["/var/log/tomcat6/catalina.out"]
}
```

Using this input we're collecting all the events from the /↵ var/log/tomcat6/catalina.out log file. Let's look at some of the events available.

Listing 5.42: A Tomcat log entry

```
Dec 27, 2012 3:51:41 AM jenkins.↵
  InitReactorRunner$1 onAttained
INFO: Completed initialization,
```

These look like fairly typical log entries that we'll be able to parse and make use of but looking into the log file we also find that we've got a number of stack traces and a number of blank lines too. The stack traces are multi-line events that we're going to need to parse into one event. We're also going to want to get rid of those blank lines rather than have them create blank events in Logstash. So it looks like we're going to need to do some filtering.

Handling blank lines with drop

First we're going to use a new filter called drop to get rid of our blank lines. The drop filter drops events when a specific regular expression match is made. Let's look at a drop filter in combination with Logstash's conditional configuration syntax for removing blank lines:

NOTE In previous Logstash releases we'd have used the grep filter to perform this same action. This filter is now community managed and does not ship with Logstash.

Listing 5.43: A drop filter for blank lines

```
if [type] == "tomcat" and [message] !~ /(.+)/ {
  drop { }
}
```

Here we're matching events with a type of tomcat to ensure we parse the right events. We're also using a regular expression match on the message field. For this match we're ensuring that the message field isn't empty. So what happens to incoming events?

- If the event does not match, i.e. the message field *is not* empty, then the event is ignored.
- If the event does match, i.e. the message field *is* empty then the event is passed to the drop filter and dropped.

The conditional syntax is very simple and useful for controlling the flow of events and selecting plugins to be used for selected events. It allows for the typical conditional if/else if/else statements, for example:

Listing 5.44: Examples of the conditional syntax

```
if [type] == "apache" {
    grok {

        . . .

    }
} else if [type] != "tomcat" {
    grok {

        . . .

    }
} else {
    drop { }
}
```

Each conditional expression supports a wide variety of operators, here we've used the equal and not equal (== and !=↵) operators, but also supported are regular expressions and in inclusions.

Listing 5.45: Conditional inclusion syntax

```
if "security" in [tags] {
   grok {
      . . .
   }
}
```

Here we've looked inside the tags array for the element
security and passed the event to the grok plugin if it's
found.

And as we've already seen conditional expressions allow
and statements as well as or, xand and xor statements.

Finally we can group conditionals by using parentheses and
nest them to create conditional hierarchies.

TIP We'll see conditional syntax a few more times
in the next couple of chapters as we filter and output
events. You can find full details of their operations at
http://www.logstash.net/docs/latest/configuration.

Handling multi-line log events

Next in our logs we can see a number of Java exception stack
traces. These are multi-line events but currently Logstash is
parsing each line as a separate event. That makes it really
hard to identify which line belongs to which exception and

make use of the log data to debug our issues. Thankfully Logstash has considered this problem and we have a way we can combine the disparate events into a single event.

To do this we're going to build some simple regular expression patterns combined with a special codec called multiline. Codecs are used inside other plugins to handle specific formats or codecs, for example the JSON event format Logstash itself uses is a codec. Codecs allow us to separate transports, like Syslog or Redis, from the serialization of our events. Let's look at an example for matching our Java exceptions as raised through Tomcat.

Listing 5.46: Using the multiline codec for Java exceptions

```
file {
  type => "tomcat"
  path => [ "/var/log/tomcat6/catalina.out" ]
  codec => multiline {
    pattern => "(^\d+\serror)|(^.+Exception: .+)↵
      |(^\s+at .+)|(^\s+... \d+ more)|(^\s*Caused ↵
      by:.+)"
    what => "previous"
  }
}
```

NOTE You can see a full list of the available codecs at http://www.logstash.net/docs/latest/.

With this file plugin containing the multiline codec we're

gathering all events in the `catalina.out` log file. We're then running these events through the `multiline` codec. The `pattern` option provides a regular expression for matching events that contain stack trace lines. There are a few variations on what these lines look like so you'll note we're using the | (which indicates `OR`) symbol to separate multiple regular expressions. For each incoming event Logstash will try to match the `message` line with one of these regular expressions.

If the line matches any one of the regular expressions, Logstash will then merge this event with either the previous or next event. In the case of our stack traces we know we want to merge the event with the event prior to it. We configure this merge by setting the `what` option to `previous`.

NOTE Any event that gets merged will also have a tag added to it. By default this tag is `multiline` but you can customize this using the `multiline_tag` option of the codec.

Let's see an example of the `multiline` codec in action. Here are two events that are part of a larger stack trace. This event:

Listing 5.47: A Java exception

```
1) Error injecting constructor, java.lang.↵
  NoClassDefFoundError: hudson/plugins/git/browser↵
  /GitRepositoryBrowser at hudson.plugins.backlog.↵
  BacklogGitRepositoryBrowser$DescriptorImpl.<init↵
  >(BacklogGitRepositoryBrowser.java:104)
```

Followed by this event:

Listing 5.48: Another Java exception

```
1 error
    at com.google.inject.internal.↵
      ProviderToInternalFactoryAdapter.get(↵
      ProviderToInternalFactoryAdapter.java:52)
...
```

When these events are processed by the `multiline` codec they will match one of the regular expression patterns and be merged. The resulting event will have a `message` field much like:

Listing 5.49: A multiline merged event

```
message => "Error injecting constructor, java.lang↵
  .NoClassDefFoundError: hudson/plugins/git/↵
  browser/GitRepositoryBrowser at hudson.plugins.↵
  backlog.↵
  BacklogGitRepositoryBrowser$DescriptorImpl.<init↵
  >(BacklogGitRepositoryBrowser.java:104)\n1 error↵
   at com.google.inject.internal.↵
  ProviderToInternalFactoryAdapter.get(↵
  ProviderToInternalFactoryAdapter.java:52). . ."
tags => [ 'multiline' ]
```

Further events that appear to be part of the same trace will continue to be merged into this event.

Grokking our Java events

Now we've cleaned up our Tomcat log output we can see what useful data we can get out of it. Let's look at our Java exception stack traces and see if we can extract some more useful information out of them using grok.

Handily there's a built-in set of patterns for Java events so let's build a grok filter that uses them:

Listing 5.50: A grok filter for Java exception events

```
if [type] == "tomcat" and "multiline" in [tags] {
  grok {
    match => [ "message", "%{JAVASTACKTRACEPART}" ←
    ]
  }
}
```

Our new grok filter will be executed for any events with a type of tomcat and with the tag of multiline. In our filter we've specified the built-in pattern JAVASTACKTRACEPART← which tries to match classes, methods, file name and line numbers in Java stack traces.

Let's see what happens when we run the stack trace we just merged through the grok filter. Our message field is:

Listing 5.51: Our Java exception message

```
message => "Error injecting constructor, java.lang←
  .NoClassDefFoundError: hudson/plugins/git/←
  browser/GitRepositoryBrowser at hudson.plugins.←
  backlog.←
  BacklogGitRepositoryBrowser$DescriptorImpl.<init←
  >(BacklogGitRepositoryBrowser.java:104)\n1 error←
  at com.google.inject.internal.←
  ProviderToInternalFactoryAdapter.get(←
  ProviderToInternalFactoryAdapter.java:52). . ."
```

Adding our grok filter we get the following fields:

Listing 5.52: Grokked Java exception

```
{
  . . .
  "class"=> "com.google.inject.internal.↵
  ProviderToInternalFactoryAdapter",
  "method"=> "get",
  "file"=> "ProviderToInternalFactoryAdapter.java"↵
  ,
  "line"=> "52",
  . . .
}
```

Let's look at our final Logstash filtering workflow for our Tomcat log events:

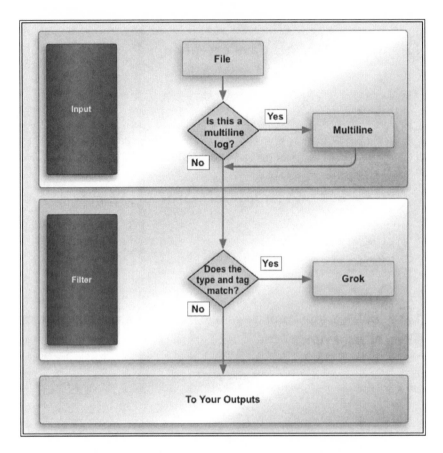

Figure 5.4: Tomcat log event workflow

We can see that we've added some useful fields with which to search or identify specific problem pieces of code. The combination of our stack trace events, this data and the ability centrally review all Tomcat logs will make it much easier for the teams that manage these applications to troubleshoot problems.

TIP All the filters in Logstash currently executes as a

`worker` model. Each worker receives an event and applies all filters, in order, before sending that event to the output plugins. If you are doing intensive filtering or discover that filtering is a bottleneck in your environment you can add additional workers by starting Logstash with the `-w` flag. You can specify the number of workers you wish to run, for example for 5 workers specify `-w 5`.

Parsing an in-house custom log format

All of the log entries we've seen up until now have been fairly standard or at least from applications that are commonly used: Apache, Postfix and Java. What happens if you have a custom application with a log format that is unusual or esoteric?

We're going to build a Grok filter for an in-house application called Alpha that is managed by your internal application support team. Alpha is used by the Finance team at Example.com and its log format does not match anything you've seen before. Let's look at an Alpha log entry:

Listing 5.53: Alpha log entry

```
1388290083+EST The Alpha server has terminated /←
  opt/alpha/server/start.vb#134 ALF13-36B AlphaApp←
  /2.4.5a/QA Release
1388290083+EST The Alpha server has started /opt/←
  alpha/server/start.vb#156 ALF13-3AA AlphaApp←
  /2.4.5a/QA Release
1388290084+EST Alpha logging has initiated /opt/←
  alpha/logging/log.vb#14 ALF02-11F AlphaApp/2.4.5←
  a/QA Release
```

You don't know much about the application but you can extrapolate a bit from the log entries you can see. Firstly, you've got a timestamp. It appears to be seconds since epoch also known as Unix time with what looks like a time zone suffixed to it. We've also got a series of log messages, what looks to be the file and line that generated the message, a log entry ID and some application identification data.

The application support team tell you that in order to troubleshoot Alpha they need:

- The timestamp.
- The log message.
- The ID of the message.
- The file and line number that generated the error.
- The name of the application.
- The version of the application.
- The release of the application.
- They also want to have a field called environment created and set to QA if the application is a QA release.

So we know we need to design a Grok filter that will extract this information from our log entries and potentially some other filters to manipulate this data further.

So firstly we're going to collect our Alpha log entries. We're going to use our smoker.example.com host which runs Ubuntu and the Logstash agent so we can just add a new file input plugin like so to our shipper.conf:

Listing 5.54: File input for our Alpha logs

```
input {
  file {
    type => "alpha"
    path => ["/opt/alpha/logs/alpha.log"]
    tags => [ "alpha", "finance" ]
  }
}
```

Here we're grabbing entries from the /opt/alpha/logs/↩ alpha.log log file. We're marking those entries with a type of alpha and tagging them with the tags alpha and finance. The tags will help us keep our log entries in order and make parsing decisions later on.

We know now we've got these logs that we need to add a grok filter to actually turn our log entry into a usable event. Let's look a single entry and start to construct a regular expression that will provide our application support team with the data they need.

Listing 5.55: Single Alpha log entry

```
1388290083+0200 The Alpha server has terminated /↵
  opt/alpha/server/start.vb#134 ALF13-36B AlphaApp↵
  /2.4.5a/QA Release
```

To extract the data we need in our Grok filter we're going to use a mix of inbuilt patterns and the named capture capability. We saw named captures earlier in this chapter. They allow you to specify a field name and a regular expressions to extract that field from the log entry.

TIP I also strongly recommend making use of regular expression tools like Rubular and the incredibly useful Grok debugger to construct your Grok filters.

Let's look at a Grok filtering statement I've prepared for our Alpha log entry already.

Listing 5.56: A Grok regular expression for Alpha

```
(?<timestamp>[\d]+)\+(?<tz>[\w]{3})\s(?<msg>.*)\s↵
  %{UNIXPATH:file}\#%{POSINT:line}\s%{GREEDYDATA: ↵
  id}\s%{WORD:appname}\/(?<appver>[\d.\d.\d\w]+)↵
  \/(?<apprelease>[\w\s]+)
```

I constructed this line by placing my sample log entry into the Grok debugger and then slowly constructing each field using named capture regular expressions or patterns as you can see here:

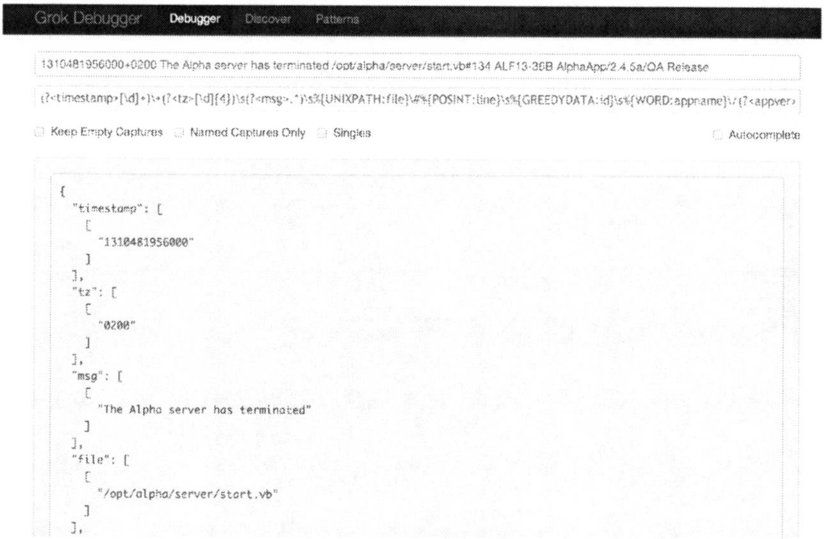

Figure 5.5: The Grok debugger at work

Shortly we'll be using this statement as the expression portion of the `match` option of a `grok` filter. In the expression we can see that we've worked through the Alpha log entry and we're extracting the following fields:

- timestamp - The Unix epoch timestamp
- tz - The timezone
- msg - The application log message
- file - The file that generated it
- line - The line of the file
- id - The log entry ID
- appname - The name of the application logging
- appver - The version of the application
- apprelease - The release of the application

Each field is generated using either an existing pattern or a named capture. For example the appname field is generated using the WORD pattern, %{WORD:appname}. Whilst the appver field is matched using a named capture: (?<appver↵>[\d.\d.\d\w]+).

Now let's add a grok filter with our Alpha match to filter these incoming events:

Listing 5.57: Alpha grok filter

```
filter {
  if [type] == "alpha" {
    grok {
      match => [ "message", "(?<timestamp>[\d]+)↵
        \+(?<tz>[\w]{3})\s(?<msg>.*)\s%{UNIXPATH:↵
        file}\#%{POSINT:line}\s%{GREEDYDATA:id}\s↵
        %{WORD:appname}\/(?<appver>[\d.\d.\d\w]+)↵
        \/(?<apprelease>[\w\s]+)" ]
      add_tag => [ "grokked" ]
    }
  }
}
```

We've added another grok filter to our filter block. We've first specified a conditional matching the type with a value of alpha. This will ensure our grok filter only matches on Alpha-related events. We've then specified the grok filter with the match option which matches a field of our log entry, here the default message field, with the expression we've just created.

But we're not quite finished yet. We know we've got a Unix

epoch timestamp and we'd like to make sure our event's @timestamp uses the right time. So let's add a date filter to our filter block.

Listing 5.58: Alpha date filter

```
filter {
  if [type] == "alpha" {
    grok {
      . . .
    }
    date {
      match => [ "timestamp", "UNIX" ]
      timezone => tz
      add_tag => [ "dated" ]
    }
  }
}
```

Here we're specified date filter and told it to update the @timestamp field to the value from the timestamp field. We've specified UNIX to indicate the timestamp field is in Unix epoch time and we're also taking into consideration the timezone we've extracted from the log entry. We've also added the tag dated to our event to indicate we updated the @timestamp.

Next we also need to create our new environment field. This field will have a value of qa if the application is a QA release or production if not. We're going to use another conditional, this one nested, to achieve this.

Listing 5.59: Alpha environment field

```
filter {
  if [type] == "alpha" {
    grok {
      . . .
    }
    date {
      ...
    }
  }
  if [apprelease] == "QA Release" {
    mutate {
      add_field => [ "environment", "qa" ]
    }
  }
  else {
    mutate {
      add_field => [ "environment", "production" ]
    }
  }
}
```

You can see that we've nested another conditional inside our existing statement. We're testing to see if the apprelease↵ field has a value of QA Release. If it does we're using a new filter called mutate that allows you to change the content of fields: convert their type, join/split fields, gsub field names amongst other capabilities. The mutate filter will add a new field called environment with a value of qa. If the apprelease field has any other value then the environment field will be set to `production`.

Finally, we've had some complaints from the application support team that the line number of the file that generated the error isn't an integer. This makes some of their debugging tools break. So we need to ensure that the `line` field has a type of integer. To do this we can again use the `mutate` filter.

Listing 5.60: Setting the line field to an integer

```
filter {
  if [type] == "alpha" {
    . . .
    mutate {
      convert => [ "line", "integer" ]
    }
  }
}
```

You can see that we've specified the `mutate` filter again and used the `convert` option to convert the `line` field into an integer.

Now when we run Logstash we should start to see our Alpha log events rendered in a format that our application support team can use. Let's look at a filtered Alpha log entry now.

Listing 5.61: A filtered Alpha event

```
{
  . . .
  @timestamp => "Sun, 29 Dec 2013 04:08:03",
  "tags" => [ "alpha", "grokked", "finance", "↵
    dated" ],
  "timestamp" => "1388290083",
  "tz" => "EST",
  "msg" => "The Alpha server has terminated",
  "file" => "/opt/alpha/server/start.vb",
  "line" => 134,
  "id" => "ALF13-36B",
  "appname" => "AlphaApp",
  "appver" => "2.4.5a",
  "apprelease" => "QA Release",
  "environment" => "qa",
  . . .
}
```

We can see that our entry contains the data our team needs and should now be searchable and easy for them to use to debug the Alpha application.

You can see that the grok filter combined with the huge variety of other available filters make this a simple and easy process. You can apply this workflow to any custom log event you need to parse.

Summary

In this chapter we've seen some of the power of Logstash's filtering capabilities. But what we've seen in this chapter is just a small selection of what it is possible to achieve with Logstash. There's a large collection of additional filter plugins available. Filters that allow you to:

TIP In addition to the plugins that ship with Logstash there are also a number of community contributed plugins available at https://github.com/elasticsearch/logstash-contrib.

- Mutate events. The mutate filter allows you to do general mutations to fields. You can rename, remove, replace, and modify fields in your events.
- Checksum events. This checksum filter allows you to create a checksum based on a part or parts of the event. You can use this to de-duplicate events or add a unique event identifier.
- Extract key value pairs. This lets you automatically parse log events that contain key value structures like foo=bar. It will create a field with the key as the field name and the value as the field value.
- Do GeoIP and DNS lookups. This allows you to add geographical or DNS metadata to events. This can be helpful in adding context to events or in processes like fraud detection using log data.
- Calculate ranges. This filter is used to check that certain fields are within expected size or length ranges.

This is useful for finding anomalous data.

- Extract XML. This filter extracts XML from events and constructs an appropriate data structure from it.
- The split filter allows you to split multi-line messages into separate events.
- The anonymize filter is useful for anonymizing fields by replacing their values with a consistent hash. If you're dealing with sensitive data this is useful for purging information like user ids, SSNs or credit card numbers.
- Execute arbitrary Ruby code. This allows you to process events using snippets of Ruby code.

TIP One of the more annoying aspects of filter patterns is that it is time consuming to test your patterns and ensure they don't regress. We've already seen the the Grok Debugger but it's also possible to write RSpec tests for your filtering patterns that can make development much simpler.

Now we've gotten a few more log sources into Logstash and our events are more carefully catalogued and filtered. In the next chapter we are going to look at how to get information, alerts and metrics out of Logstash.

Chapter 6

Outputting Events from Logstash

In the previous chapters we've seen some of the output plugins available in Logstash: for example Redis, Syslog, ElasticSearch. But in our project we've primarily focussed on moving events from agents to our central server and from our central server to ElasticSearch. Now, at this stage of the project, we want to start using some of the other available output plugins to send events or generate actions from events. We've identified a list of the top outputs we need to create:

- Send alerts for events via email.
- Send alerts for events via instant messaging.
- Send alerts through to a monitoring system.
- Collect and deliver metrics through a metrics engine.

Let's get started with developing our first output.

Send email alerts

The first needed output we've identified is alerts via email. Some parts of the IT team really want to get email notifications for certain events. Specifically they'd like to get email notifications for any stack traces generated by Tomcat. To do this we'll need to configure the email output plugin and provide some way of identifying the stack traces we'd like to email.

Updating our multiline filter

Since we've just tackled this log source in Chapter 5 we're going to extend what we've already done to provide this capability. Let's first look at our existing multiline codec:

Listing 6.1: The Tomcat multiline file input and codec

```
file {
  type => "tomcat"
  path => [ "/var/log/tomcat6/catalina.out" ]
  codec => multiline {
    pattern => "(^\d+\serror)|(^.+Exception: .+)↵
      |(^\s+at .+)|(^\s+... \d+ more)|(^\s*Caused ↵
      by:.+)"
    what => "previous"
  }
}
```

The file input and multiline codec will match any message lines with the pattern specified and merge them into one event. It'll also add the tag `multiline` to the event.

Configuring the email output

Next we need to configure our `email` plugin in the `output` block.

Listing 6.2: The email output plugin

```
if [type] == "tomcat" and "multiline" in [tags] {
  email {
    body => "Triggered in: %{message}"
    subject => "This is a Logstash alert for ↵
      Tomcat stack traces."
    from => "logstash.alert@example.com"
    to => "appteam@example.com"
    via => "sendmail"
  }
}
```

Our `email` output plugin is configured to only match events with the `type` of `tomcat` and with the tag `multiline`. This way we don't flood our mail servers with every event by mistake.

NOTE You can see this and a full list of the `email` outputs options at http://www.logstash.net/docs/latest/outputs/email.

We then specify the body of the email in plain text using the body option. We're sending the message:

Listing 6.3: The content of our email

```
"Triggered in: %{message}"
```

The body of the email will contain the specific stack trace which is contained in the message field. The email output also has support for HTML output which you can specify using the htmlbody option.

NOTE We've referred to the message field via Logstash's sprintf format. We've prefixed it with a percentage sign and enclosed the field in braces. You can see more details at http://www.logstash.net/docs/latest/configuration.

We've also specified the subject of the email using the subject option.

We next specify the from and to options that set the emission and destination email addresses. And lastly we set the via option which controls how the email is sent: either sendmail or smtp. In our case we're using sendmail which directly calls the MTA locally on the host. If needed, you can also control a variety of other email options including SSL/TLS and authentication using the options directive.

Email output

Now every time Logstash receives a Java exception stack trace the `email` output will be triggered and the stack trace will be emailed to the `appteam@example.com` address for their attention.

Figure 6.1: Java exception email alert

WARNING Please be aware that if you get a lot of stack traces this could quickly become an unintentional email-based Denial of Service attack.

Send instant messages

Our next output is similar to our email alert. Some of your colleagues in the Security team want more immediate alerting of events and would like Logstash to send instant messages when failed SSH logins occur for sensitive hosts. Thanks to the work we did earlier in the project, documented in Chapter 3, we're already collecting the syslog events from /var/log/secure on our sensitive hosts using the following file input:

Listing 6.4: The file input for /var/log/secure

```
file {
  type => "syslog"
  path => ["/var/log/secure", "/var/log/messages"]
  exclude => ["*.gz"]
}
```

Identifying the event to send

As we've already got the required event source now all we need to do is identify the specific event on which the Security team wants to be alerted:

Listing 6.5: Failed SSH authentication log entry

```
Dec 28 21:20:27 maurice sshd[32348]: Failed ←
  password for bob from 184.75.0.187 port 32389 ←
  ssh2
```

We can see it is a standard Syslog message. Our Security team wants to know the user name and the source host name or IP address of the failed login. To acquire this information we're going to use a grok filter:

Listing 6.6: Failed SSH authentication grok filter

```
if [type] == "syslog" {
  grok {
    match => [ "message", "%{SYSLOGBASE} Failed ↵
    password for %{USERNAME:user} from %{↵
    IPORHOST:host} port %{POSINT:port} %{WORD:↵
    protocol}" ]
    add_tag => [ "ssh", "grokked", "auth_failure" ↵
    ]
  }
}
```

Which, when it matches the Syslog log entry, should produce an event like this:

Listing 6.7: Failed SSH authentication Logstash event

```
{
  "message" => "Dec 28 21:20:27 maurice sshd↵
    [32348]: Failed password for bob from ↵
    184.75.0.187 port 32389 ssh2",
  "@timestamp" => "2012-12-28T21:20:27.016Z",
  "@version" => "1",
  "host" => "maurice.example.com",
  "timestamp" => "Dec 28 21:20:27",
  "logsource" => "maurice.example.com",
  "program" => "sshd",
  "pid" => "32348",
  "user" => "bob",
  "host" => "184.75.0.187",
  "port" => "32389",
  "protocol" => "ssh2",
  "tags" => [
     [0] "ssh",
     [1] "grokked",
     [2] "auth_failure"
  ]
}
```

You can see that our grok filter has matched the event using the specified pattern and populated the fields: timestamp, logsource, program, pid, port, protocol and most importantly user and host. The event has also been tagged with the ssh, grokked and ssh_auth_failure tags.

Sending the instant message

We now have a tagged event with the data our Security team needs. How do we get it to them? To do this we're going to use a new output plugin called xmpp that sends alert notifications to a Jabber/XMPP user.

Listing 6.8: The xmpp output plugin

```
if "ssh_auth_failure" in [tags] and [type] == "↵
  syslog" {
  xmpp {
    message => "Failed login for user %{user} from↵
      %{host} on server %{logsource}"
    user => "alerts@jabber.example.com"
    password => "password"
    users => "security@example.com"
  }
}
```

The xmpp output is simple to configure. First, to ensure only the right events are alerted, we've specified that the output only triggers on events tagged with ssh_auth_failure and with a type of syslog. Next, we've defined a message that contains the data our security team wants by referencing the fields we created in our grok filter earlier. Lastly, we've specified the connection details: user, password and an array of users to be alerted about these events.

WARNING Here we're using an internal XMPP network inside our organization. Remember, if you are using a public

XMPP network, to be careful about sending sensitive data across that network.

Now when a failed SSH login occurs and Logstash matches the appropriate event an instant message will be generated:

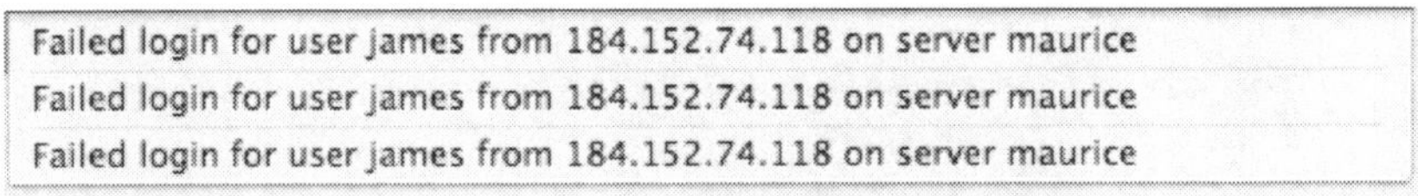

```
Failed login for user james from 184.152.74.118 on server maurice
Failed login for user james from 184.152.74.118 on server maurice
Failed login for user james from 184.152.74.118 on server maurice
```

Figure 6.2: Jabber/XMPP alerts

NOTE You can see this and a full list of the xmpp output's options at http://www.logstash.net/docs/latest/outputs/xmpp.

Send alerts to Nagios

Our previous two outputs have been alerts and very much point solutions. Our next output is an integration with an external framework, in this case with the monitoring tool Nagios. Specifically we're going to generate what Nagios calls "passive checks" from our log events and send them to a Nagios server.

Nagios check types

There are two commonly used types of Nagios checks: active and passive. In an active check Nagios initiates the check from a Nagios server using a plugin like check_icmp or check_http. Alternatively, passive checks are initiated outside Nagios and the results sent to a Nagios server. Passive checks are usually used for services that are:

- Asynchronous in nature and cannot be monitored effectively by polling their status on a regularly scheduled basis.
- Located behind a firewall and cannot be checked actively from the Nagios server.

Identifying the trigger event

We're going to generate some of these Nagios passive checks using a new output plugin called nagios.

Let's look at a log event that we'd like to trigger a Nagios passive service check: a STONITH cluster fencing log event.

Listing 6.9: A STONITH cluster fencing log event

```
Dec 18 20:24:53 clunode1 clufence[7397]: <notice> ↵
  STONITH: clunode2 has been fenced!
```

Assuming we've got an input plugin that picks up this event, we start by identifying and parsing this specific event via a grok filter.

Listing 6.10: Identify Nagios passive check results

```
if [type] == "syslog" {
  grok {
    match => [ "message", "%{SYSLOGBASE} <notice> ↵
      STONITH: %{IPORHOST:cluster_node} has been ↵
      fenced!" ]
    add_tag => [ "nagios_check" ]
    add_field => [
      "nagios_host", "%{cluster_node}",
      "nagios_service", "cluster"
    ]
  }
}
```

We're searching for events with a type of syslog and with a pattern match to our STONITH cluster fence event. If the event matches we're adding a tag called nagios_check and we're adding two fields, nagios_host and nagios_service. This will tell the nagios output the hostname and service on which it should alert.

Parsing our example log entry will result in event tags and fields that look like:

Listing 6.11: The grokked STONITH event

```
{
  "message" => "Dec 18 20:24:53 clunode1 clufence↩
    [7397]: <notice> STONITH: clunode2 has been ↩
    fenced!",
  "@timestamp" => "2013-12-18T20:24:53.965Z",
  "@version" => "1",
  "host" => "clunode1",
  "timestamp" => "Dec 18 20:24:53",
  "logsource" => "clunode1",
  "program" => "clufence",
  "pid" => "7397",
  "cluster_node" => "clunode2",
  "nagios_host" => "clunode2",
  "nagios_service" => "cluster",
  "tags" => [
    [0] "nagios_check",
  ]
}
```

The nagios output

To output this event as a Nagios passive check we specify the nagios output plugin.

Listing 6.12: The Nagios output

```
if "nagios_check" in [tags] {
  nagios { }
}
```

Nagios can receive passive checks in several ways. The nagios output plugin takes advantage of Nagios' external command file. The external command file is a named pipe from which Nagios listens periodically for incoming commands. The nagios output generates PROCESS_SER-VICE_CHECK_RESULT commands and submits them to this file.

NOTE For external commands to be processed you must have the check_external_commands=1 option set in your Nagios server configuration.

The nagios output checks events for the tag nagios_check and if it exists then submits a PROCESS_SERVICE_CHECK_RESULT↵ command to the Nagios external command file containing details of the event. It's important to remember that the user running Logstash must be able to write to the Nagios command file. The output assumes the external command file is located at /var/lib/nagios3/rw/nagios.cmd but this can be overridden with the commandfile option:

Listing 6.13: The Nagios output with a custom command file

```
nagios {
  tags => "nagios_check"
  command file => "/var/run/nagios/rw/nagios.cmd"
}
```

TIP If your Nagios server is not located on the same host you can make use of the `nagios_nsca` output which provides passive check submission to Nagios via NSCA.

The Nagios external command

Let's look at the command generated by Logstash.

Listing 6.14: A Nagios external command

```
[1357065381] EXTERNAL COMMAND: ↵
  PROCESS_SERVICE_CHECK_RESULT;clunode2;cluster;2;↵
  file://maurice.example.com/var/log/rhcluster/↵
  stonith.log: Jul 18 20:24:53 clunode1 clufence↵
  [7397]: <notice> STONITH: clunode2 has been ↵
  fenced!
```

We can see the host and service name we specified in the `nagios_host` and `nagios_service` fields, `clunode2` and `cluster` respectively. We can also see the Nagios return code, 2, which indicates this is a CRITICAL event. By default the nagios output sends passive check results with a status of CRITICAL. You can override this in two ways:

- Set a field on the event called nagios_level with a value of the desired state: OK, WARNING, CRITICAL, or UNKNOWN.
- Use the nagios_level option in the output to hardcode a status.

Setting the nagios_level field will override the nagios_level↵ configuration option.

NOTE You can see this and a full list of the nagios outputs options at http://www.logstash.net/docs/latest/outputs/nagios.

The Nagios service

On the Nagios side you will need a corresponding host and service defined for any incoming command, for example:

Listing 6.15: A Nagios service for cluster status

```
define service {
  use  local-service
  host_name  clunode2
  service_description  cluster
  active_checks_enabled  0
  passive_checks_enabled  1
  notifications_enabled  1
  check_freshness  0
  check_command  check_dummy
}
```

Now when a matching event is received by Logstash it will be sent as an external command to Nagios, then processed as a passive service check result and trigger the cluster service on the clunode2 host. It's easy to extend this to other events related to specific hosts and services for which we wish to monitor and submit check results.

Outputting metrics

One of the key needs of your colleagues in both Operations and Application Development teams is the ability to visually represent data about your application and system status and performance. As a mechanism for identifying issues and understanding performance, graphs are a crucial tool in every IT organization. During your review of Logstash as a potential log management tool, you've discovered that one of the really cool capabilities of Logstash is its ability to collect and send metrics from events.

But there are lots of tools that do that right? Not really. There are lots of point solutions designed to pick up one, two or a handful of metrics from infrastructure and application specific logs and deliver them to tools like Graphite or through brokers like StatsD. Logstash instead allows you to centralize your metric collection from log events in one tool. If a metric exists in or can be extrapolated from a log event then you can deliver it to your metrics engine. So for your next output we're going to take advantage of this capability and use Logstash events to generate some useful metrics for your environment.

Logstash supports output to a wide variety of metrics engines and brokers including Ganglia, Riemann, Graphite, StatsD, MetricCatcher, and Librato, amongst others.

Collecting metrics

Let's take a look at how this works using some of the log events we're collecting already, specifically our Apache log events. Using the custom log format we created in Chapter 5 our Apache log servers are now logging events that look like:

Listing 6.16: JSON format event from Apache

```
{
  "host" => "host.example.com",
  "path" => "/var/log/httpd/logstash_access_log",
  "tags" => [ "wordpress", "www.example.com" ],
  "message" => "50.116.43.60 - - [22/Dec↵
    /2012:16:09:30 -0500] \"GET / HTTP/1.1\" 200 ↵
    4979",
  "timestamp" => "2012-12-22T16:09:30-0500",
  "clientip" => "50.116.43.60",
  "duration" => 11313,
  "status" => 200,
  "request" => "/index.html"
  "urlpath" => "/index.html",
  "urlquery" => "",
  "method" => "GET",
  "bytes" => 4979,
  "vhost" => "www"
  "@timestamp"=>"2012-12-22T16:09:30.658Z",
  "@version => "1",
  "type"=>"apache"
}
```

We can already see quite a few things we'd like to graph based on the data we've got available. Let's look at some potential metrics:

- An incremental counter for response status codes: 200, 404, etc.
- An incremental counter for method types: GET, POST,

etc.

- A counter for the bytes served.
- A timer for the duration of each request.

StatsD

To create our metrics we're going to use the statsd output. StatsD is a tool written by the team at Etsy. You can read about why and some more details about how StatsD works at http://codeascraft.com/2011/02/15/ measure-anything-measure-everything/. It acts as a front-end broker to Graphite and is most useful because you can create new metrics in Graphite just by sending it data for that metric. I'm not going to demonstrate how to set up StatsD or Graphite. There are a number of excellent guides, HOWTOs, Puppet modules and Chef cookbooks for that online.

NOTE If you don't want to use StatsD you can send metrics to Graphite directly using the graphite output.

Setting the date correctly

Firstly, getting the time accurate really matters for metrics so we're going to use the date filter we used in Chapter 5 to ensure our events have the right time. Using the date filter we will set the date and time our Apache events to the value of the timestamp field contained in each event:

Listing 6.17: The Apache event timestamp field

```
"timestamp": "2012-12-22T16:09:30-0500"
```

Let's add our date filter now:

Listing 6.18: Getting the date right for our metrics

```
if [type] == "apache" {
  date {
    match => [ "timestamp", "ISO8601" ]
    add_tag => [ "dated" ]
  }
}
```

Our date filter has a conditional wrapper that checks for a type of apache to ensure it only matches our Apache events. It then uses the match statement to specify that Logstash should look for an ISO8601 format in the field timestamp. This will ensure our event's timestamp will match the timestamp of the original Apache log event. We're also adding the tag dated to mark events which have had their timestamps set.

NOTE Remember date matching uses Java's Joda-Time library.

The StatsD output

Now we've got the time of our events correct we're going to use the statsd output to create the metrics we would like from our Apache logs:

Listing 6.19: The statsd output

```
if [type] == "apache" {
  statsd {
    increment => "apache.status.%{status}"
    increment => "apache.method.%{method}"
    count => [ "apache.bytes", "%{bytes}" ]
    timing => [ "apache.duration", "%{duration}" ]
  }
}
```

You can see we're only matching events with a type of apache. You could also match using tags, excluding tags or using fields. Next we've specified two incremental counters, a normal counter and a timer.

Our first two incremental counters are:

Listing 6.20: Incremental counters

```
increment => "apache.status.%{status}"
increment => "apache.method.%{method}"
```

They use the increment option and are based on two fields we've specified in our Apache log events: status and method, which track the Apache response status codes and the HTTP methods respectively. Our metrics are named with a prefix of apache. and make use of Graphite's namespaces, each . representing a folder in Graphite's views.

Each event will either create a new metric, if that status or method doesn't already have a metric, or increment an existing metric. The result will be a series of metrics matching each status:

Listing 6.21: Apache status metrics in Graphite

```
apache.status.200
apache.status.403
apache.status.404
apache.status.500
. . .
```

And each method:

Listing 6.22: Apache method metrics in Graphite

```
apache.method.GET
apache.method.POST
. . .
```

Each time an Apache log event is received by our Logstash central server it will trigger our output and increment the relevant counters. For example a request using the GET method with a 200 response code Logstash will send an update to StatsD for the apache.method.GET and apache.status.200 metrics incrementing them by 1.

StatsD will then push the metrics and their data to Graphite and produce graphs that we can use to monitor our Apache web servers.

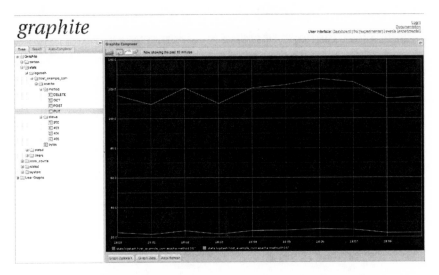

Figure 6.3: Apache status and method graphs

Here we can see our Apache method metrics contained in the Graphite namespace: stats -> logstash -> host_example_-com -> apache -> method. The namespace used defaults to logstash but you can override this with the namespace option.

Our counter metric is similar:

Listing 6.23: The apache.bytes counter

```
count => [ "apache.bytes", "%{bytes}" ]
```

We're creating a metric using the count option called apache.bytes and when an event comes in we're incrementing that metric by the value of the bytes field in that event.

We can then see this graph presented in Graphite:

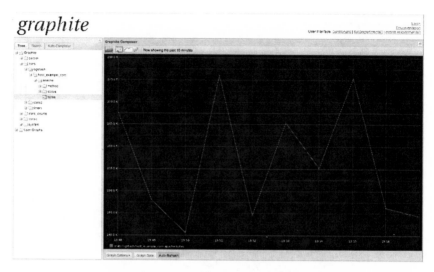

Figure 6.4: Apache bytes counter

The last metric creates a timer, using the `timing` option, based on the `duration` field of our Apache log event which tracks the duration of each request.

Listing 6.24: The apache.duration timer

```
timing => [ "apache.duration", "%{duration}" ]
```

We can also see this graph, together with the automatic creation of lower and upper bounds metrics, as well as mean and sum metrics:

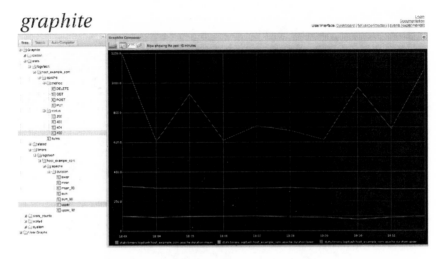

Figure 6.5: Apache request duration timer

Sending to a different StatsD server

By default, the `statsd` output sends results to the `localhost` on port 8125 which is the default port on which StatsD starts. You can override this using the `host` and `port` options.

Listing 6.25: The StatsD output with a custom host and port

```
if [type] == "apache" {
  statsd {
    host => "statsd.example.com"
    port => 8130

    . . .

  }
}
```

NOTE You can see this and a full list of the `statsd` output's options at http://www.logstash.net/docs/latest/outputs/statsd.

Now we have a useful collection of basic graphs from our Apache events. From this we can add additional metrics from our Apache events or from other log sources.

NOTE Also available in Logstash 1.1.6 and later is the `metrics` filter which is a useful shortcut to creating metrics from events. For some purposes it should ultimately replace the approach described here for gathering and generating metrics.

Summary

We've now configured a small collection of initial outputs for our logging project that provide alerts, monitoring and metrics for our environment. It's easy to extend these outputs and add further outputs from the wide collection available.

With these outputs configured we've got events coming in, being filtered and outputted in a variety of ways. Indeed Logstash is becoming an important tool in our monitoring and management toolbox. As a result of the growing importance of Logstash we now need to consider how to ensure it stays up and scales to meet demand. In the next chapter we're going to learn how to grow our Logstash environment.

Chapter 7

Scaling Logstash

One of the great things about Logstash is that it is made up of easy to fit together components: Logstash itself, Redis as a broker, Elasticsearch and the various other pluggable elements of your Logstash configuration. One of the significant fringe benefits of this approach is the ease with which you can scale Logstash and those components.

We're going to scale each of the pieces we introduced and installed in Chapter 3. Those being:

- Redis - Which we're using as a broker for incoming events.
- Elasticsearch - Which is handling search and storage.
- Logstash - Which is consuming and indexing the events.

This is a fairly basic introduction to scaling these components with a focus on trying to achieve some simple objectives:

- To make Logstash as redundant as possible with no single points of failure.

- To avoid messages being lost in transit from inputs and outputs.
- To make Logstash perform as well as possible.

WARNING As with all scaling and performance management this solution may not work for your environment or fully meet your requirements. Our introduction will show you the basics of making Logstash more resilient and performant. From there you will need to monitor and tune Logstash to achieve the precise results you need.

Our final scaled architecture will look like this:

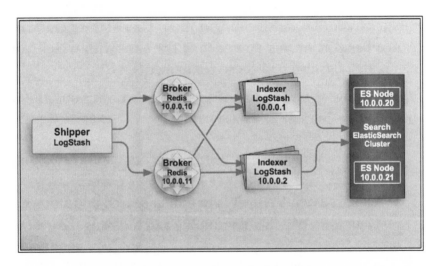

Figure 7.1: Logstash Scaled Architecture

TIP As with its installation, scaling Logstash is significantly easier and more elegant using tools like Puppet or Chef. Again setting up either is beyond the scope of this book but there are several Puppet modules for Logstash on the Puppet Forge and a Chef cookbook. These either support some minimal scaling or can be adapted to deliver these capabilities.

Scaling Redis

In our implementation we're using Redis as a broker between our Logstash agents and the Logstash central server. One of the reasons we chose Redis is that it is very simple. Thankfully making Redis redundant is also simple. Logstash can send events to and receive events from multiple Redis instances in a failover configuration.

It's important to note that this is a failover rather than true high availability. Events are not "round robin'ed" or load balanced between Redis instances. Logstash will try to connect to a Redis instance and send events. If that send succeeds then it will continue to send events to that Redis instance. If the send fails then Logstash will select the next Redis instance and try to send to it instead.

This does, however, provide you with some basic redundancy for your broker through the deployment of additional Redis instances but has limited impact if your Redis instance is a performance bottleneck for your environment. If this is an issue for you then you can designate Redis instances for specific agents or groups of agents with additional Redis instances defined if you'd like redundancy.

TIP You could also try other brokers like AMQP or zeroMQ.

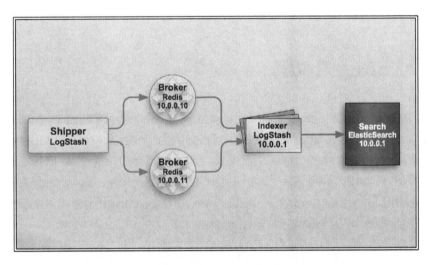

Figure 7.2: Logstash Redis failover

We're already running one Redis server, currently running on our Logstash central server, so we're going to do three things to make our environment a bit more redundant:

- Create two new Redis instances on separate hosts.
- Configure Logstash to write to and read from both Redis instances.
- Turn off the Redis instance on our central server.

NOTE Other options for providing scalability with Redis include a client-side proxy such as nutcracker and the forthcoming support for Redis clustering.

Installing new Redis instances

Let's spin up two new Ubuntu hosts:

Redis host #1

- Hostname: midnighttoker.example.com
- IP Address: 10.0.0.10

Redis host #2

- Hostname: spacecowboy.example.com
- IP Address: 10.0.0.11

To install new Redis instances we replicate the steps from Chapter 3. Again we can either install Redis via our packager manager or from source. On our Ubuntu hosts we install it from a package as that's simple:

Listing 7.1: Installing Redis

```
$ sudo apt-get install redis-server
```

Now we need to ensure Redis is bound to an external interface. To do this we need to edit the /etc/redis/redis.←
conf configuration file and bind it to a single interface, our

two hosts' respective external IP addresses: `10.0.0.10` and `10.0.0.11`:

Listing 7.2: Binding Redis to the external interface

```
bind 10.0.0.10
```

Repeat this for our second host replacing `10.0.0.10` with `10.0.0.11`.

Now Redis is configured, we can start the Redis instances on both hosts:

Listing 7.3: Start the Redis instances

```
$ sudo /etc/init.d/redis-server start
```

Test Redis is running

We can test if the Redis instances are running by using the `redis-cli` command on each host.

Listing 7.4: Test Redis is running

```
$ redis-cli -h 10.0.0.10
redis 10.0.0.10:6379> PING
PONG
```

Now repeat on our second host.

Configuring Redis output to send to multiple Redis servers

As we've discussed the redis output supports the ability to specify multiple Redis instances in a failover model and send events to them. We're going to configure the redis output on each of our shipping agents with our two new Redis instances. To do this we'll need to update the configuration in our /etc/logstash/conf.d/shipper.conf file:

Listing 7.5: Multi instance Redis output configuration

```
output {
  redis {
    host => [ "10.0.0.10", "10.0.0.11" ]
    shuffle_hosts => true
    data_type => "list"
    key => "logstash"
  }
}
```

TIP If you find yourself having performance issues with Redis you can also potentially make use of the `threads` option. The `threads` option controls the number of threads you want the input to spawn. This is the same as declaring the input multiple times.

You can see we've specified an array of IP addresses in our host option. We've also specified an option called shuffle_hosts which will shuffle the list of hosts when Logstash starts. This means Logstash will try one of these Redis instances and if it connects it will send events to that instance. If the connection fails it will try the next instance in the list and so on until it either finds an instance that receives events or runs out of instances and fails.

To enable this we'll also need to restart Logstash.

Listing 7.6: Restarting the Logstash agent for Redis

```
$ sudo service logstash restart
```

Configuring Logstash to receive from multiple Redis servers

Now that Logstash is potentially sending events to multiple Redis instances we need to make sure it's checking all of those instances for events. To do this we're going to update our /etc/logstash/conf.d/central.conf configuration file on our central Logstash server like so:

Listing 7.7: Multiple Redis instances

```
input {
  redis {
    host => "10.0.0.10"
    data_type => "list"
    type => "redis-input"
    key => "logstash"
  }
  redis {
    host => "10.0.0.11"
    data_type => "list"
    type => "redis-input"
    key => "logstash"
  }
}
```

You can see we've added two redis input plugins to our input stanza: one for each Redis instance. Each is identical except for the IP address for the Redis instance. Now when Logstash starts it will connect to both instances and wait for events.

To enable these inputs we'll need to restart Logstash.

Listing 7.8: Restart the Logstash agent

```
$ sudo service logstash restart
```

Testing our Redis failover

Let's test that our Redis failover is working. Firstly, let's stop one of our Redis instances.

Listing 7.9: Stopping a Redis instance

```
midnighttoker$ sudo /etc/init.d/redis-server stop
```

You should see an error message appear very shortly afterward on our central Logstash server:

Listing 7.10: Redis connection refused exception

```
{:message=>"Input thread exception", :plugin=>#<↵
  LogStash::Inputs::Redis:0x1b5ca70 @db=0, @key="↵
  logstash", @threadable=true, type="redis-input",↵
  @host="10.0.0.10", . . . :exception=> #<Redis::↵
  CannotConnectError: Error connecting to Redis on↵
  10.0.0.10:6379 (ECONNREFUSED)>, . . . :level=>:↵
  warn}
```

TIP You should add checks for Redis to your monitoring environment. If you use Nagios or similar tools there are a number of plugins like this and this that can help.

Now stop our second Redis instance.

Listing 7.11: Stopping a second Redis instance

```
spacecowboy$ sudo /etc/init.d/redis-server stop
```

And a similar log message will appear for this instance on our central Logstash server.

We'll also be able to see that log events have stopped flowing from our remote agents:

Listing 7.12: Remote agent event sending failures

```
{:message=>"Failed to send event to redis" . . .
```

Now you should be able to start one of our Redis instances and see events flowing through to Logstash from your remote agents. Now start and stop the Redis instances to see the remote agents switch between them and send through to the central server.

Shutting down our existing Redis instance

Finally, we need to shut down our existing Redis instance on our central Logstash server: smoker. Let's stop the service and ensure it's turned off.

Listing 7.13: Shut down Redis

```
$ sudo /etc/init.d/redis-server stop
```

Now ensure it won't get started again:

Listing 7.14: Stop Redis starting

```
$ sudo update-rc.d redis-server disable
```

Now we've got some simple failover capability for our Redis broker. We've also got Redis running on a dedicated pair of hosts rather than on our central server. Next we can look at making our Elasticsearch environment a bit more scalable.

Scaling Elasticsearch

Elasticsearch is naturally very amenable to scaling. It's easy to build new nodes and Elasticsearch supports both unicast and multicast clustering out of the box with very limited configuration required. We're going to create two new Ubuntu hosts to run Elasticsearch on and then join these hosts to the existing cluster.

Elasticsearch host #1

- Hostname: grinner.example.com
- IP Address: 10.0.0.20

Elasticsearch host #2

- Hostname: sinner.example.com
- IP Address: 10.0.0.21

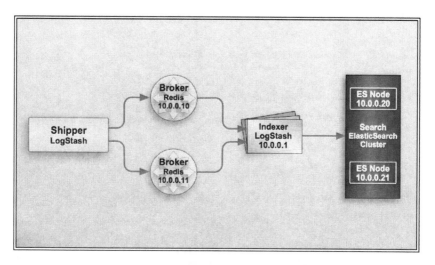

Figure 7.3: Elasticsearch scaling

Installing additional Elasticsearch hosts

Firstly, we need to install Java as a prerequisite to Elastic-search.

Listing 7.15: Installing Java for Elasticsearch

```
$ sudo apt-get install openjdk-7-jdk
```

We also have DEB packages for Elasticsearch that we can use on Ubuntu. We can download from the Elasticsearch download page.

Listing 7.16: Download Elasticsearch

```
$ wget https://download.elasticsearch.org/↵
  elasticsearch/elasticsearch/elasticsearch-1.0.0.↵
  deb
```

We then install it including first telling Elasticsearch where to find our Java JDK installation by setting the JAVA_HOME environment variable.

Listing 7.17: Install Elasticsearch

```
$ export JAVA_HOME=/usr/lib/jvm/java-7-openjdk-↵
  i386/
$ sudo dpkg -i elasticsearch-1.0.0.deb
```

Repeat this process for both hosts.

Configuring our Elasticsearch cluster and new nodes

Next we need to configure our Elasticsearch cluster and node name. Remember that new Elasticsearch nodes join any cluster with the same cluster name they have defined. So we want to customize our cluster and node names to ensure our new nodes join the right cluster. To do this we need to edit the /etc/elasticsearch/elasticsearch.yml file. Look for the following entries in the file:

Listing 7.18: Elasticsearch cluster and node names

```
# cluster.name: elasticsearch
# node.name: "Franz Kafka"
```

We're going to uncomment and change both the cluster and node name on each new host. We're going to choose a cluster name of logstash and a node name matching each new host name.

Listing 7.19: Grinner cluster and node names

```
cluster.name: logstash
node.name: "grinner"
```

Then:

Listing 7.20: Sinner cluster and node names

```
cluster.name: logstash
node.name: "sinner"
```

We then need to restart Elasticsearch to reconfigure it.

Listing 7.21: Restarting Elasticsearch to reconfigure

```
$ sudo /etc/init.d/elasticsearch restart
```

We can then check Elasticsearch is running and has joined the cluster by checking the Cluster Health API like so:

Listing 7.22: Checking the cluster status.

```
$ curl -XGET 'http://10.0.0.20:9200/_cluster/↵
  health?pretty=true'
{
  "cluster_name" : "logstash",
  "status" : "green",
  "timed_out" : false,
  "number_of_nodes" : 4,
  "number_of_data_nodes" : 3,
  "active_primary_shards" : 30,
  "active_shards" : 60,
  "relocating_shards" : 0,
  "initializing_shards" : 0,
  "unassigned_shards" : 0
```

NOTE That's weird. Four nodes? Where did our fourth node come from? That's Logstash itself which joins the cluster as a client. So we have three data nodes and a client node.

We can see that our cluster is named logstash and its status is green. Green means all shards, both primary and replicas are allocated and functioning. A yellow cluster status will mean that only the primary shards are allocated, i.e. the cluster has not yet finished replication across its nodes. A red cluster status means there are shards that are not allocated.

This clustering takes advantage of Elasticsearch's multicast clustering, which is enabled by default. So any hosts we add to the cluster must be able to find the other nodes via multicast on the network. You could instead use unicast networking and specify each node. To do this see the `discovery.zen.ping.unicast.hosts` option in the `/etc↩/elasticsearch/elasticsearch.conf` configuration file. Also available is an EC2 discovery plugin if you are running in Amazon EC2.

Monitoring our Elasticsearch cluster

Using the command line API is one way of monitoring the health of your Elasticsearch cluster but a far better method is to use one of the several plugins that are designed to do this. Plugins are add-ons for Elasticsearch that can be installed via the `plugin` tool. We're going to choose a cluster monitoring plugin called Paramedic written by Karel Minarik. Let's install it on our `grinner` host:

Listing 7.23: Installing Paramedic

```
grinner$ sudo /usr/share/elasticsearch/bin/plugin ↩
  -install \
karmi/elasticsearch-paramedic
```

With the plugin installed we can now browse to the following URL:

Listing 7.24: The Paramedic URL

```
http://10.0.0.20:9200/_plugin/paramedic/index.html
```

From here we can see a display of both the current cluster state and a variety of performance, index and shard metrics that looks like this:

Figure 7.4: The Paramedic Elasticsearch plugin

There are several other similar plugins like BigDesk and Head.

NOTE There are also Nagios plugins that can help you monitor Elasticsearch.

Managing Elasticsearch data retention

One of the other key aspects of managing Elasticsearch scaling and performance is working out how long to retain your log data. Obviously this is greatly dependent on what you use the log data for, as some data requires longer-term retention than other data.

TIP Some log data, for example financial transactions, need to be kept for all time. But does it need to be searchable and stored in Elasticsearch forever? Probably not. In which case it is easy enough to output certain events to a different store like a file from Logstash for example using the `file` output plugin. This becomes your long-term storage and if needed you can also send your events to shorter-term storage in Elasticsearch.

Deleting unwanted indexes

Logstash by default creates an index for each day, for example `index-2012.12.31` for the day of 12/31/2012. You can keep these indexes for as long as you need (or you have disk space to do so) or set up a regular "log" rotation. To do this you can use Elasticsearch's own Delete API to remove older indexes, for example using `curl`:

Listing 7.25: Deleting indexes

```
$ curl -XDELETE http://10.0.0.20:9200/logstash-↵
  2012.12.31
```

Here we're deleting the `logstash-2012.12.31` index. You can easily automate this, for example this ticket contains an example Python script that deletes old indexes. We've reproduced it at `http://logstashbook.com/code/7/logstash_ index_cleaner.py` too. Another example is a simple Bash script found at `https://github.com/cnf/logstash-tools/ blob/master/elasticsearch/clean-elasticsearch.sh`. Additionally the recently introduced Curator tool (see Curator section below) can also make managing LogStash indexes very simple.

Using any of these you can set up an automated regime to remove older indexes to match whatever log retention cycle you'd like to maintain.

Optimizing indexes

It's also a good idea to use Elasticsearch's optimize function to optimize indexes and make searching faster. You can do this on individual indexes:

Listing 7.26: Optimizing indexes

```
$ curl -XPOST 'http://10.0.0.20:9200/logstash-↵
  2013.01.01/_optimize'
```

Or on all indexes:

Listing 7.27: Optimizing all indexes

```
$ curl -XPOST 'http://10.0.0.20:9200/_optimize'
```

It's important to note that if your indexes are large that the optimize API call can take quite a long time to run. You can see the size of a specific index using the Elasticsearch Indices Stats API like so:

Listing 7.28: Getting the size of an index

```
$ curl 'http://10.0.0.20:9200/logstash-2012.12.31/↵
  _stats?clear=true&store=true&pretty=true'
. . .
  "total" : {
    "store" : {
      "size" : "110.5mb",
      "size_in_bytes" : 115965586,
      "throttle_time" : "0s",
      "throttle_time_in_millis" : 0
    }
  }
}
. . .
```

TIP There are also some simple community tools for working with Elasticsearch and Logstash that you might find handy at https://github.com/cnf/logstash-tools/tree/master/elasticsearch.

Curator

More recently to support managing Logstash indexes the Elasticsearch team has released a tool called Curator. Curator helps you automate the process of deleting, optimizing and manage indexes on your Elasticsearch cluster.

Listing 7.29: Installing curator

```
$ sudo pip install elasticsearch-curator
```

TIP Curator works best with Elasticsearch 1.0 or later. If you're running Logstash 1.4.0 or later this is the version you should have. If you use an earlier version of Elasticsearch you can try Curator 0.6.2. You can install it via `pip` also like so: `pip install elasticsearch-curator==0.6.2`.

Curator installs a binary called `curator` onto your host. It allows you to manage Elasticsearch indexes. For example, to delete indexes.

Listing 7.30: Deleting indexes with Curator

```
$ curator --host 10.0.0.20 -d 30
```

This will delete indexes older than thirty days, specified using the `-d` flag, on our `10.0.0.20` host.

Curator can also optimize indexes and close indexes. Closing indexes is highly useful when you need to keep indexes for a while but don't need to search them, for example you might need to keep 30 days of logs but only search the last 7 days. This ensures optimal performance of your Logstash instance as closed indexes only occupy space and don't get searched when you query your data. This ensures your queries are fast and limited only to the data you need. To close indexes you would run:

Listing 7.31: Closing indexes using Curator

```
$ curator --host 10.0.0.20 -c 7
```

This will close all indexes older than 7 days.

To see the full list of Curator's capabilities run it with the -h flag.

Listing 7.32: Getting Curator help

```
$ curator -h
```

You can also find a blog post showing more of Curator's capabilities at http://untergeek.com/2014/02/18/curator-managing-your-logstash-and-other-time-series-indices and you can find the Curator source code at https://github.com/elasticsearch/curator.

More Information

Elasticsearch scaling can be a lot more sophisticated than I've been able to elaborate on here. For example, we've not examined the different types of Elasticsearch node we can define: allowing nodes to be cluster masters, to store or not store data, or to act as "search load balancers." Nor have we discussed hardware recommendations or requirements.

There are a variety of other sources of information, including this excellent video and this post about how to scale Elasticsearch and you can find excellent help on the #↵ elasticsearch IRC channel on Freenode or the Elasticsearch mailing list.

TIP A common, and worth calling out specifically, Elasticsearch problem at scale is the number of open files. Elasticsearch opens a lot of files and sometimes can hit the `nofile` limit of your distribution. The Elasticsearch team have written an article that talks about how to address this issue.

Scaling Logstash

Thus far we've got some redundancy in our Redis environment and we've built an Elasticsearch cluster but we've only got a single Logstash indexer receiving events from Redis and passing them to Elasticsearch. This means if something happens to our Logstash indexer then Logstash stops working. To reduce this risk we're going to add a second Logstash indexer to our environment running on a new host.

Logstash host #1

- Hostname: smoker.example.com
- IP Address: 10.0.0.1

Logstash host #2

- Hostname: picker.example.com
- IP Address: 10.0.0.2

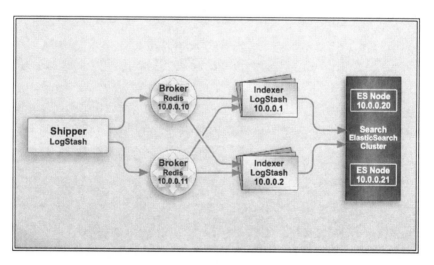

Figure 7.5: Logstash indexer scaling

Creating a second indexer

To create a second indexer we need to replicate some of the steps from Chapter 3 we used to set up our initial Logstash indexer.

Listing 7.33: Setting up a second indexer

```
picker$ wget -O - http://packages.elasticsearch.↵
  org/GPG-KEY-elasticsearch | sudo apt-key add -
picker$ sudo sh -c "echo 'deb http://packages.↵
  elasticsearch.org/logstash/1.4/debian stable ↵
  main' > /etc/apt/sources.list.d/logstash.list"
picker$ sudo apt-get update
picker$ sudo apt-get install logstash
smoker$ sudo scp /etc/logstash/conf.d/central.conf↵
  bob@picker:/etc/logstash/conf.d
```

You can see we've added the Logstash repository and installed the Logstash package and copied the existing smoker central.conf configuration file. We're all set up and ready to go. The best thing is that we don't even need to make any changes to our existing Logstash configuration.

Now let's start our new Logstash instance. Edit the `/etc/default/logstash' file and change the line:

Listing 7.34: The stock /etc/default/logstash file

```
START=no
```

to:

Listing 7.35: The updated /etc/default/logstash file

```
START=yes
```

You can then run the Logstash service.

Listing 7.36: Starting the central Logstash server

```
picker$ sudo service logstash start
```

So what happens now? As both Logstash indexers are using the same configuration and both are listening for inputs from the same Redis brokers they will start to both process events. You'll see some events being received on each Logstash instance. Assuming they have the same configuration (you are using configuration management by now right?) then the events will be processed the same way and pass into our Elasticsearch cluster to be stored. Now if something goes wrong with one Logstash instance you will have a second functioning instance that will continue to process. This model is also easy to scale further and you can add additional Logstash instances as needed to meet performance or redundancy requirements.

Summary

As you can see, with some fairly simple steps that we've made our existing Logstash environment considerably more resilient and provided some additional performance capacity. It's not quite perfect and it will probably need to be tweaked as we grow but it provides a starting point to expand upon as our needs for additional resources increase.

In the next chapter we'll look at how we can extend Logstash to add our own plugins.

Chapter 8

Extending Logstash

One of the awesome things about Logstash is that there are so many ways to get log events into it, manipulate and filter events once they are in and then push them out to a whole variety of destinations. Indeed, at the time of writing, there were nearly 100 separate input, filter and output plugins. Every now and again though you encounter a scenario where you need a new plugin or want to customize a plugin to better suit your environment.

TIP The best place to start looking at the anatomy of Logstash plugins are the plugins themselves. You'll find examples of inputs, filters and outputs for most purposes in the Logstash source code repository.

Now our project has almost reached its conclusion we've decided we better learn how to extend Logstash ourselves to cater for some of the scenarios when you need to modify or create a plugin.

WARNING This introduction is a simple, high-level introduction to how to extend Logstash by adding new plugins. It's not a definitive guide to writing or learning Ruby.

Anatomy of a plugin

Let's look at one of the more basic plugins, the `stdin` input, and see what we can learn about plugin anatomy.

Listing 8.1: The stdin input plugin

```
require "logstash/inputs/base"
require "logstash/namespace"
require "socket"

class LogStash::Inputs::Stdin < LogStash::Inputs::↵
 Base
    config_name "stdin"
    milestone 3

    default :codec, "line"

    public
    def register
      @host = Socket.gethostname
    end # def register

    def run(queue)
      while true
        begin
          data = $stdin.sysread(16384)
          @codec.decode(data) do |event|
            decorate(event)
            event["host"] = @host
            queue << event
          end
        rescue EOFError, LogStash::ShutdownSignal
          break
        end
      end # while true
      finished
```

A Logstash plugin is very simple. Firstly, each plugin requires the Logstash module:

Listing 8.2: Requiring the Logstash module

```
require 'logstash/namespace'
```

And then the Logstash class related to the type of plugin, for example for an input the LogStash::Inputs::Base class:

Listing 8.3: Requiring the LogStash::Inputs::Base class

```
require 'logstash/inputs/base'
```

For filters we require the LogStash::Filters::Base↩ class and outputs the LogStash::Outputs::Base class respectively.

We also include any prerequisites, in this case the stdin input requires the Socket library for the gethostname method.

Each plugin is contained in a class, named for the plugin type and the plugin itself, in this case:

Listing 8.4: The plugin class

```
class LogStash::Inputs::Stdin < LogStash::Inputs::↩
  Base
```

We also include the prerequisite class for that plugin into our plugin's class, < LogStash::Inputs::Base.

Each plugin also requires a name and a milestone provided by the config_name and milestone methods. The config_name provides Logstash with the name of the plugin. The milestone sets the status and evolutionary state of the plugin. Valid statuses are 0 to 3 where 0 is unmaintained, 1 is alpha, 2 is beta and 3 is production. Some milestones impact how Logstash interacts with a plugin, for example setting the status of a plugin to 0 or 1 will prompt a warning that the plugin you are using is either not supported or subject to change without warning.

Every plugin also has the register method inside which you should specify anything needed to initialize the plugin, for example our stdin input sets the host name instance variable.

Each type of plugin then has a method that contains its core execution:

- For inputs this is the run method, which is expected to run forever.
- For filters this is the filter method. For outputs this is the receive method.

So what happens in our stdin input? After the register method initializes the plugin then the run method is called. The run method takes a parameter which is the queue of events. In the case of the stdin input the loop inside this method is initiated. The input then runs until stopped, processing any incoming events from STDIN using the to_event method.

One last method is defined in our stdin input, teardown↵ . When this method is specified then Logstash will execute it when the plugin is being shutdown. It's useful for cleaning up, in this case closing the pipe, and should call the finished method when it's complete.

Creating our own input plugin

Now we've got a broad understanding of how a plugin works let's now create one of our own. We're going to start with a simple plugin to read lines from a named pipe: a poor man's file input. First let's add our requires and create our base class.

Listing 8.5: The namedpipe framework

```
require 'logstash/namespace'
require 'logstash/inputs/base'

class LogStash::Inputs::NamedPipe < LogStash::↵
  Inputs::Base
  . . .
end
```

We've added requires for an input and a class called LogStash::Inputs::NamedPipe. Now let's add in our plugin's name and status using the config_name and milestone methods. We're also going to specify the default codec, or format, this plugin will expect events to arrive in. We're going to specify the plain codec as we expect our events to be text strings.

Listing 8.6: The namedpipe framework plugin options

```ruby
require 'logstash/namespace'
require 'logstash/inputs/base'

class LogStash::Inputs::NamedPipe < LogStash::↵
 Inputs::Base
   config_name "namedpipe"
   milestone 1
   default :codec, "line"

   # The pipe to read from
   config :pipe, :validate => :string, :required ↵
     => true


   . . .
end
```

You can see we've also added a configuration option, using the `config` method. This method allows us to specify the configuration options and settings of our plugins, for example if we were configuring this input we could now use an option called `pipe`:

Listing 8.7: The namedpipe input configuration

```
input {
    namedpipe {
        pipe => "/tmp/ournamedpipe"
        type => "pipe"
    }
}
```

Configuration options have a variety of properties: you can validate the content of an option, for example we're validating that the `pipe` option is a `string`. You can add a default for an option, for example `:default => "default option↵"`, or indicate that the option is required. If an option is required and that option is not provided then Logstash will not start.

Now let's add the guts of the `namedpipe` input.

Listing 8.8: The namedpipe input

```ruby
require 'logstash/namespace'
require 'logstash/inputs/base'

class LogStash::Inputs::NamedPipe < LogStash::↵
 Inputs::Base
   config_name "namedpipe"
   milestone 1
   default :codec, "line"
   config :pipe, :validate => :string, :required ↵
     => true

   public
   def register
     @logger.info("Registering namedpipe input", ↵
       :pipe => @pipe)
   end

   def run(queue)
     @pipe = open(pipe, "r+")
     @pipe.each do |line|
       line = line.chomp
       host = Socket.gethostname
       path = pipe
       @logger.debug("Received line", :pipe => ↵
         pipe, :line => line)
       e = to_event(line, host, path)
       if e
         queue << e
       end
     end
   end
```

We've added three new methods: `register`, `run`, and `teardown`.

The `register` method sends a log notification using the `@logger` instance variable. Adding a log level method, in this case `info` sends an information log message. We could also use `debug` to send a debug-level message.

The `run` method is our queue of log events. It opens a named pipe, identified using our `pipe` configuration option. Our code constructs a source for our log event, that'll eventually populate the `host` and `path` fields in our event. We then generate a debug-level event and use the `to_event` method to take the content from our named pipe, add our host and path and pass it to Logstash as an event. The `run` method will keep sending events until the input is stopped.

When the input is stopped the `teardown` method will be run. This method closes the named pipe and tells Logstash that the input is finished.

Let's add our new plugin to Logstash and see it in action.

Adding new plugins

Adding new plugins to Logstash is done by specifying a plugin directory and loading plugins when Logstash starts. To do this we specify some plugins directories and load our plugins from those directories. Let's start by creating those plugins directories.

Listing 8.9: Creating plugins directories

```
$ sudo mkdir -p /etc/logstash/{inputs,filters,↵
  outputs}
```

Here we've created three directories under our existing /↵
etc/logstash directory, one directory for each type of plugin: inputs, filters and outputs. You will need to do this on every Logstash host that requires the custom plugin.

Logstash expects plugins in a certain directory structure: logstash/type/plugin_name.rb. So for our namedpipe input we'd place it into:

Listing 8.10: Adding the namedpipe input

```
$ sudo cp namedpipe.rb /etc/logstash/inputs
```

Now our plugin is in place we can start Logstash and specify the --pluginpath command line flag, for example to start Logstash on our central server we'd run:

Listing 8.11: Running Logstash with plugin support

```
$ /opt/logstash/bin/logstash agent --verbose \
-f /etc/logstash/conf.d/central.conf \
--log /var/log/logstash/logstash.log --pluginpath ↵
  /etc/
```

The --pluginpath command line flag specifies the root of the directory containing the plugin directories, in our case /etc/.

Now if we start Logstash we should be able to see our `namedpipe` input being registered:

Listing 8.12: Registering the namedpipe input

```
Input registered {:plugin=>#<LogStash::Inputs::↵
  NamedPipe:0x163abd0 @add_field={}, . . .
```

NOTE You should also update your Logstash init script to add the `--pluginpath` command line flag.

Writing a filter

Now we've written our first input let's look at another kind of plugin: a filter. As we've discovered filters are designed to manipulate events in some way. We've seen a variety of filters in Chapter 5 but we're going to write one of our own now. In this filter we're going to add a suffix to all `message` fields. Let's start by adding the code for our filter:

Listing 8.13: Our suffix filter

```
require "logstash/filters/base"
require "logstash/namespace"

class LogStash::Filters::AddSuffix < LogStash::↵
 Filters::Base
    config_name "addsuffix"
    milestone 1

    config :suffix, :validate => :string

    public
    def register
    end

    public
    def filter(event)
      if @suffix
        msg = event["message"] + " " + @suffix
        event["message"] = msg
      end
    end
end
```

Let's examine what's happening in our filter. Firstly, we've required the prerequisite classes and defined a class for our filter: LogStash::Filters::AddSuffix. We've also named and set the status of our filter, the experimental addsuffix filter, using the config_name and milestone methods.

We've also specified a configuration option using the

config method which will contain the suffix which we will be adding to the event's message field.

Next, we've specified an empty register method as we're not performing any registration or plugin setup. The most important method, the filter method itself, takes the event as a parameter. In our case it checks for the presence of the @suffix instance variable that contains our configured suffix. If no suffix is configured the filter is skipped. If the suffix is present it is applied to the end of our message and the message returned.

TIP If you want to drop an event during filtering you can use the event.cancel method.

Now we can configure our new filter, like so:

Listing 8.14: Configuring the addsuffix filter

```
filter {
  addsuffix {
    suffix => "ALERT"
  }
}
```

If we now run Logstash we'll see that all incoming events now have a suffix added to the message field of ALERT resulting in events like so:

Listing 8.15: An event with the ALERT suffix

```
{
  "host" => "smoker.example.com",
  "@timestamp" => "2013-01-21T18:43:34.531Z",
  "message" => "testing ALERT",
  "type" => "human"
}
```

You can now see how easy it is to manipulate events and their contents.

Writing an output

Our final task is to learn how to write the last type of plugin: an output. For our last plugin we're going to be a little flippant and create an output that generates CowSay events. First, we need to install a CowSay package, for example on Debian-distributions:

Listing 8.16: Installing CowSay on Debian and Ubuntu

```
$ sudo apt-get install cowsay
```

Or via a RubyGem:

Listing 8.17: Installing CowSay via a RubyGem

```
$ sudo gem install cowsay
```

This will provide a cowsay binary our output is going to use. Now let's look at our CowSay output's code:

Listing 8.18: The CowSay output

```ruby
require "logstash/outputs/base"
require "logstash/namespace"

class LogStash::Outputs::CowSay < LogStash::↵
 Outputs::Base
  config_name "cowsay"
  milestone 1

  config :cowsay_log, :validate => :string, :↵
    default => "/var/log/cowsay.log"

  public
  def register
  end

  public
  def receive(event)
    msg = `cowsay #{event["message"]}`
    File.open(@cowsay_log, 'a+') { |file| file.↵
      write("#{msg}") }
  end

end
```

Our output requires the prerequisite classes and creates a class called LogStash::Outputs::CowSay. We've specified the name of the output, cowsay with config_name method and marked it as an alpha release with the milestone of 1. We've specified a single configuration option using the config method. The option, cowsay_log specifies a default log file location, /var/log/cowsay.log, for our log output.

Next we've specified an empty register method as we don't have anything we'd like to register.

The guts of our output is in the receive method which takes an event as a parameter. In this method we've shell'ed out to the cowsay binary and parsed the event["message"] (the contents of the message field) with CowSay. It then writes this "cow said" message to our /var/log/cowsay.log file.

We can now configure our cowsay output:

Listing 8.19: Configuring the cowsay output

```
output {
  cowsay {}
}
```

You'll note we don't specify any options and use the default destination. If we now run Logstash we can generate some CowSay statements like so:

Figure 8.1: Cow said "testing"

You can see we have an animal message. It's easy to see how you can extend an output to send events or portions of events to a variety of destinations.

Summary

This has been a very simple introduction to writing Logstash plugins. It gives you the basics of each plugin type and how to use them. You can build on these examples easily enough and solve your own problems with plugins you've developed yourself.

Index

Thanks! I hope you enjoyed the book.

ISBN 978-0-9888202-2-7

CPSIA information can be obtained at www.ICGtesting.com
Printed in the USA
BVOW07s2210010315

389875BV00001B/47/P